Praise for *Yoga for the Brain*!

"I love *Yoga for the Brain*! It is a great way to relax, unwind, and play. **Even better, research shows that games like these can have a mind-body benefit no matter how old you are. Sign me up for more!**"
—*Camille Leon, Founder, Holistic Chamber of Commerce*

"Never before have I seen such a book, with word search puzzles, secret messages, and even more for the reader to enjoy! More than just a word search puzzle book, it's also packed with facts and information. Sitting down with the book is a great way to relax and stretch those brain muscles. I can see why the puzzles are considered 'yoga for the brain'! **This book is highly recommended for those looking for puzzles, relaxation, inspiration, and enjoyment!**"
—*Carla Trueheart for* Readers' Favorite

"*Yoga for the Brain* is inspirational, relevant, and fun! The puzzles are challenging in a good way, and the messages are insightful and meaningful. **It's well worth your time. I highly recommend it to everyone looking for something uniquely uplifting.** It provides an all-around positive experience anyone can benefit from. The books encompass food for thought and food for the soul!"
—*Brenda Krueger Huffman, Publisher,* Women's Voices Magazine

"Cristina Smith's **fun and easily accessible works brilliantly blend quantum consciousness-based science with profound philosophical wisdom.**"
—*Dr. Amit Goswami, Quantum Physicist and bestselling author of* The Self-Aware Universe

"While I've never actually heard the term 'yoga for the brain' before, it makes total sense. This book easily fulfills the mental and spiritual aspects of a yoga practice. **So much more than a puzzle book, the fun facts, history, and education lining the pages make** *Yoga for the Brain* **books a unique treasure.** I highly recommend it for an entertaining and enlightening experience!"
—*Sheri Hoyte for* Reader Views

"Everything Cristina writes about in her books is about our choice of what to do with the great gift of life we have been given. She has experienced in her own life the power of the spirit to transform her life and allow her to tap into her energy and enthusiasm to help others become all they can be. Puzzles are half of what these books are about. The other half is the commentary Cristina provides that helps us to learn to live fully in this present moment. Highly recommended!"
—*Dr. Russell Fanelli, Professor Emeritus, Western New England University*

"Cristina Smith thinks deeply and writes with the kind of simplicity and clarity that only comes from an almost cellular attunement to her subjects. Without pretense or posturing, she uplifts me."
—*Steven Forrest, author of* The Inner Sky

"Highly Recommended!"
—*The Wishing Shelf, UK*

The *Yoga for the Brain*™ series has earned more than a dozen literary awards in the United States and United Kingdom. Have fun discovering why by looking inside!

Inspired Wisdom Word Search
Yoga for the Brain™

Cristina Smith
Rick Smith

A POST HILL PRESS BOOK
ISBN: 978-1-64293-386-4

Inspired Wisdom Word Search:
Yoga for the Brain™
© 2020 by Cristina Smith and Rick Smith
All Rights Reserved

Post Hill Press
New York • Nashville
posthillpress.com

Published in the United States of America

Table of Contents

When Is a Brain Teaser More Than an Exercise?

The book you are holding is much more than it appears. More than a quiz book or a diversion, it is an attempt to show readers their truest self through the medium of brain games.

As the Guinness Record Holder for greatest memory, I'm often asked to give my opinion on brain-training games. People always ask me if mental exercises like Sudoku or crosswords will *really* help improve their memory. My response is always the same. *It depends.*

One of the secrets of brain training is to keep pushing yourself. The brain benefits from diversity. While it's certainly fun to test your recall and trivia knowledge with *Jeopardy!* or crossword clues, true brain training comes from learning new information or from having new and different experiences. Nearly all the scientific studies on the subject point to this one truth. Brain-training games definitely have the power to enhance cognitive skills, but *it depends* on how much the brain is stimulated.

So, I challenge you, dear reader, to push yourself and go beyond your comfort zone. Whether it's tackling the most difficult-seeming puzzles, or merely trying a game outside of your usual style or favorite subject, the key is brain stimulation. Part of what makes this book so special is that it provides stimulating and fun brain games to challenge people at all ability levels.

Even more than mental stimulation, *Inspired Wisdom Word Search: Yoga for the Brain* was written to stimulate the soul. Each puzzle reveals meaningful messages about philosophy and spirituality. Those who dive deep into this adventure will feel like an ancient philosopher uncovering the secrets of life. It's an opportunity to examine the inner workings of your brain and your beliefs.

The ancient Greeks pioneered the art of deep thinking. They knew the brain was much more than just a bundle of neurons. Motivation, energy, faith, passion, wisdom, and other spiritual matters are innately tied to critical thinking, logic, and intellect. Only by going past the dogma can we see that these states are both sides of the same coin and it is spinning the truth of our lives.

Not interested in the philosophical and spiritual aspects of this book? Not to worry! You can still sharpen your memory and have fun with the brain-boosting games. For those who want a deeper, more meaningful form of entertainment, I invite you on a quest that will stimulate your brain and your soul.

—*Dave Farrow*

Inspiration Just for You

Inspiration is such a great word, isn't it? Doesn't it give you a bit of a lift just to hear it? What does it mean to you? What inspires you? Take a second. Start a list. Some surprising things may appear.

Beautiful sunsets and sunrises, a gorgeous piece of music, that perfect summer day. What about love? Family? Animal companions? The planet itself? Being of service to others, the scent of a flower, truth, beauty, and the Divine?

Inspiration can strike like lightning and often at the most unlikely times, like while walking, doing the dishes, or taking a shower. Sometimes it's a flash from the corner of the eye, a hummingbird or butterfly flits by, and then, just as suddenly, is gone.

In a culture obsessed with measuring talent, intelligence, and ability, we often overlook the important role of inspiration. It awakens us to new possibilities by allowing us to transcend our ordinary experiences and limitations. Inspiration propels a person from apathy to possibility, and transforms the way we perceive our own capabilities.

Inspiration charges us up. Gets us moving. Keeps us moving. It allows us to overcome obstacles that might otherwise stop us. Inspiration is the engine of the train; it not only keeps us on track, but is fuel for our inner fires.

We can take our inspiration beyond our bodies to our hearts, minds, and souls. It may be a momentary pleasure to enjoy, or mine it for all it is worth and turn it into a business or a painting or a lifestyle. We find it in the mundane and superlative moments of our lives from a last-minute dinner menu, to the perfect song for the moment, to the answer to a tricky problem, to a never-before-seen invention to benefit the planet.

We associate inspiration with kind of a cosmic state, don't we? An inspired speaker fires us up. Art begins with the artist becoming inspired. Successful art pieces go on to inspire others. Writing can be a great source of inspiration, from journals to published books, self-care to fiction to poetry to research. It all depends, doesn't it? A museum some may find deadly boring can be a profound source of inspiration for others.

Inspiration helps us think outside the box and be creative. And it's fun. More and more groups of people are coming together over shared inspirations, whether it's animal or planetary or ecosystem rights or the true desire to create community.

Consider your own inspiration. Look at your life and find the moments you would define as inspired. How have others in the midst of their inspiration impacted you?

We've brought together sixty examples of inspiration for your puzzle-doing pleasure. Our contributors' ages span from sixteen to eighty years old. Topics range from an immigrant story to a letter from Santa to brain science and epigenetics to cherry blossoms to healing wisdom to joy, love, abundance, hope, and magic. Mark your favorites. Notice who you agree with and who you choose to skip. The funny thing is watching how that changes over time.

Have fun with these examples of inspired wisdom. And consider your own. What would you offer if you were in this book?

Inspiration comes in many shapes, sizes, colors, and flavors. What inspires one person may be a big turn-off to another. That's the beauty of our diversity. Let these wisdoms percolate through you. See what sticks with you. Most of all, have fun!

Let's Play!

Have Fun!

How to Play

A word search puzzle consists of letters placed in a grid. Some of the letters form words, others don't. The object of this game is to find and mark all of the words hidden inside the grid that appear in the accompanying word list.

The words may be placed horizontally, vertically, or diagonally, and arranged forward or backward. They may share letters with other words.

Hidden within the puzzle is a secret message created by the letters that are not used in any word within the grid. The key to decoding it is underneath the text of the reading.

The blank lines are where you will place the letters discovered once the word-search phase of the puzzle is complete. Starting from the top-left corner of the puzzle grid and proceeding left to right, line by line, place each unused letter on the blank line in the order that it appears. When solved, an Inspired Wisdom message associated with the reading magically appears!

Cristina Smith & Rick Smith

How to Find the Words

Knowing where to start is sometimes
the key to the solution.

There is no one right way to solve these word search puzzles. It's individual. Your unique brilliance will reveal your perfect way forward. Word search puzzles are a wonderful way to play with your brain and help increase its flexibility. Experiment with these different strategies and notice how it feels when doing each. It is likely that one approach will feel more natural.

What's great about playing with your brain in this context is that it is a no-risk proposition. Nothing critical is on the line. There is no deadline. No one else will be judging your performance. It is the perfect laboratory in which to do research on yourself. A whole brain approach could look something like this:

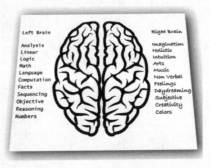

Start with the right-brain intuitive approach. Read the conversation. Scan the grid and see what words you notice first. Circle them and cross them off the list. It is interesting to make a note of the ones that pop out as an indicator of your current state of being.

Take a look at the word list and then look again at the grid and see what else reveals itself. Consider picking out a word and see if you are able to find it by shifting your perspective.

Next, move to the left-brain logical strategy. A common tactic for finding all the words is to go through the puzzle left to right (or vice versa) and look for the first letter of the word. After finding the letter, look at the eight surrounding letters to see whether the next letter of the word is there. Continue this system until the entire word is found.

The step-by-step method approaches the word list in order. It's helpful to skip over the ones that are elusive at the moment and come back to those words later.

To finish, switch on the right-brain intuitive technique again. Which words did you have a hard time finding? Notice anything interesting about them? Isn't it fascinating what we see and don't see?

**Get to know yourself in different states of mind.
New perspectives emerge.**

✤ *Cristina Smith & Rick Smith*

Colorful Tip

Many people use a pencil to circle found words and then cross or check them off the list. That works well, especially if you have a good eraser. However, the grid looks a bit chaotic when all of the word list is found. As a colorful tip, use a highlighter felt-tip pen to identify found words in the grid. It can make it easier to recognize which letters remain unused when decoding the secret message.

About the Inspired Wisdom Messages

Each puzzle includes a unique short story shared by one of our sixty inspiring contributing authors. They range in age from sixteen to eighty, offering us a slice of wisdom from diverse perspectives. After the puzzle section, you will briefly meet each author and be able to find out more about them at www.InspiredWisdomWordSearch.com.

Some keys to the mysteries of inner wisdom may be unlocked while playing with the magic of word search. These puzzles are not mind-numbingly difficult. They are designed to stretch your mind and perspective, like a yoga pose.

Each puzzle creates specific benefits. First, reading initiates the overall focus of the story. The carefully-selected word list supports different facets of the theme. Solving the puzzle itself improves whole brain health function and flexibility. Finally, the deciphered Inspired Wisdom reveals a powerful affirmation that can embed these positive messages into the essence of everyday life.

Have fun solving all of these deliciously unique puzzles and inspiring secret messages!

We Are the Fortunate Ones

Have you ever thought about how fortunate we are? Sometimes we do not fully realize our amazing good luck.

First of all, we are alive! This is a huge blessing. Our parents found each other and we were born. And we're still here to tell the tale.

Our five senses provide a lifetime of pleasure. We can enjoy peaches, popcorn, lemonade, fragrant jasmine, music, the vibrant colors of nature, the sun warming our skin, and the embrace of a loved one.

We are lucky to be alive in this century. The pharaohs of Egypt did not have the wealth we enjoy. They could die from a cut. We have antibiotics. They never left Egypt. We can fly to another continent in a matter of hours.

We can take a hot shower with no need to haul water from a well and build a fire. We enjoy light after sunset by flicking a switch.

We can read. Only recently has everyone been taught to read and books been widely available.

We are able to communicate instantly with people anywhere in the world.

We have immediate answers to many questions with the touch of button or the sound of our voice.

We have strawberries in winter, chocolate from faraway lands, and sushi without having to get up early and go fishing.

Sometimes life doesn't seem fair, and it isn't. It's good to remember that, when it gets down to basics, we truly are incredibly fortunate to be alive here and now.

—*Lisa Tansey*

Inspired Wisdom:

--- --- --- --- --- --- --- --- --- --- --- --- --- ---

--- --- --- --- --- --- --- --- --- --- --- --- --- --- --- --- ---

--- --- --- --- --- --- --- --- ---

```
T T O H A T E S N U S B K P E
C H O C O L A T E S T L I E T
C P M N I E S A H S D E A A P
O I L G A W L O S C Y S T C Y
M S H E I T A O A I A S P H G
M T U T A R U N P T L I R E E
U E C S A S S R C O I N A S F
N H T H H W U E E I D G H O O
I E P S E I R R E B W A R T S
C W D R G Y H R E I I T E E S
A L S A E N E T N T U C N R R
T R O S N W I E L N D I C N E
E I N V O O B M A A M L I Y W
L A U H E C M T R S E K S K O
T Y S Y O D E E A A S W U U L
P O P C O R N J L A W R M E F
```

Answers	Lemonade	Read
Antibiotics	Light	Shower
Blessing	Lisa	Skin
Chocolate	Loved	Strawberries
Communicate	Music	Sunset
Egypt	Nature	Sushi
Flowers	Peaches	Switch
Fortunate	Pharaohs	Tansey
Hot	Pleasure	Warming
Jasmine	Popcorn	Wealth

You Matter

Do you feel all the way down in your bones that you matter? It can be easy to get swept away in our busy world. We can forget that our actions affect others. We may feel small, insignificant, and worthless. We may feel that it is selfish to worry about ourselves. These feelings may cause us to feel hopeless and disconnected or as if our lives do not matter. This can quickly take us down into the deep, dark depths of despair and futility.

The good news is we have the power to change that. Right here. Right now. Your life matters.

Reflect on what you are grateful for and know that you make a difference. Take time to write down what you have learned each day so you can cultivate your unique gifts. Identify what you would have done differently. Look for trends and integrate your discoveries into your daily life.

Focus on what is meaningful for you. Doing that will create a ripple effect that inspires others to live fully. Become aware of how your success positively influences and encourages other people.

Trust that your unique gifts make an impact on this world every day.

Your happiness directly helps others be happy. Your inspiration inspires others. You matter!

—*Crystal Lindsey*

Inspired Wisdom:

___   ___   _____   ___
__   _____   __   ___

```
S  U  T  R  E  N  D  S  R  I  P  P  L  E  S
P  N  S  S  L  U  F  G  N  I  N  A  E  M  W
L  I  Y  E  P  O  S  I  T  I  V  E  L  Y  E
E  Q  O  I  G  L  E  A  R  N  E  D  U  A  P
H  U  P  R  R  A  G  R  A  T  E  F  U  L  T
G  E  O  E  E  E  R  B  L  I  S  C  M  Y  P
O  O  W  V  R  G  O  U  T  I  U  U  F  F  F
O  A  E  O  N  N  N  T  O  L  N  U  R  I  O
D  A  R  C  E  N  D  A  T  C  L  D  A  T  C
C  R  Y  S  T  A  L  I  H  L  N  N  S  N  U
T  I  N  I  S  P  V  I  Y  C  R  E  A  E  S
H  T  I  D  H  A  P  P  I  N  E  S  S  D  Y
G  G  I  F  T  S  T  C  A  P  M  I  O  I  N
I  T  R  E  F  L  E  C  T  R  E  T  T  A  M
R  O  S  E  C  N  E  U  L  F  N  I  A  L  L
```

Bones	Grateful	Positively
Change	Happiness	Power
Crystal	Helps	Reflect
Cultivate	Identify	Right
Discoveries	Impact	Ripple
Encourages	Influences	Swept
Focus	Learned	Trends
Fully	Lindsey	Trust
Gifts	Matter	Unique
Good	Meaningful	

Truths to Tell

Oh, the stories we make up about ourselves. So many are untrue. Some days we walk around feeling like an imposter. We feel undeserving of love. We believe we're unworthy of experiencing a rich, fulfilling life. We defer our most precious dreams for a later, *better* time.

This is no way to exist in a world filled with possibilities. There are expansive, luminous rays of hope and opportunity underneath that heap of meaningless untruths. It takes an awakening. It requires the courage to find new ways to fall in love with ourselves in all of our glorious imperfections. It takes consciously integrating self-care practices into our day to feed and grow our capacity to love ourselves and others, freely and fully.

As that love expands, our passions, purpose, and propensities begin to illuminate. To live the best and most abundant life, rewrite the script to match inner beauty. Let a new spirit and lightness frame the truth about your goodness, gifts, and grace.

Boldly step forward. Know you are on perfectly safe and sound ground. Precisely ask for and fervently pursue what you want and deserve. Those old, false stories don't belong to you. Your life force and dreams, on the other hand, are yours to wholeheartedly own, activate, and achieve.

—*Maria Dowd*

Inspired Wisdom:

— — — — —   — — — — — — — — —   — — —
— — — — — — —   — — — — — — —   — — — —   — — — —
— — — —   — — —   — — —   — — — — —   — — — — — —

```
P S U O I R O L G C B F R P A
P U R S U E V O L F O U T R B
E D R C O U R A G E L L A O O
S U W P T L I S T F D L U P T
N L A O O A I A P E L Y P E P
O N B D D S V G S I Y O E N I
I L U E G I E E H A R N T S R
S G N I T A R G E T N I L I C
S S D C T V O V U Y N U T T S
A W A K E N I N G T M E R I I
P E N S T S I H A I S V S E S
H T T S N T U I N C T E A S M
Y O O A Y U R O J A O I B Y A
A N P S H T U R T P R H D I E
N X N E E S R B E A A C U T R
E Y F R E E L Y M C R A Y S D
```

Abundant	Dreams	Maria
Achieve	Expansive	Opportunity
Activate	Freely	Passions
Awakening	Fully	Propensities
Best	Glorious	Purpose
Boldly	Hope	Pursue
Capacity	Integrating	Rays
Courage	Lightness	Script
Deserve	Love	Spirit
Dowd	Luminous	Truths

Say Yes to Life

We all have choices. To say I had an inferiority complex as a young child would be an understatement. When I decided to say yes to life, I could have just as easily said no.

After all, I had just moved to America from Italy and left behind all of my extended family, cousins, aunts, uncles, and dear friends. Starting a new life in a place where you know absolutely no one, without speaking or understanding the new language, is quite a challenge, to say the least.

But I was determined to accept this challenge. I said yes and chose to make my life an adventure. Little by little I began to make new friends and learned how to become an *Americano*.

At age eleven, I saw a friend play the drums. I had never experienced such raw excitement and thrill! I wanted to do that. Yes, I wanted to have my OWN drum set! Whatever it took. I got a job delivering newspapers to make some money. I would get up at four in the morning and do my route, even in the brutally cold winters of upstate New York.

I was in heaven when I bought my drum set. Yes! I would practice at every chance I got. I started to develop some musical chops. Music is a language everyone speaks.

When I moved to California in my twenties, my skills as a drummer came in handy. I started to meet other like-minded musicians and before you knew it, I was having the time of my life. Playing music. Saying yes. Embracing change and my new life.

Music opened up a whole new world for me. It gave me joy, confidence, and friends. I still play music every day. What's your joy? Say yes to it.

—*Gerlando Compilati*

Inspired Wisdom:

___ _____ _____ __
_____ _____ __
_____ _____

```
C T H G E I T A L I P M O C U
H Y U E C O U S I N S N I E N
O T H R I L L V E R R S A C C
P I Y L I M A F E Y L A T I L
S R O A L L A P X N G U A T E
Y O G N S N A I C I S U M C S
E I J D A P S K I L L S H A E
N R O O S C S F T M I A U R S
O E S W Y D I I E C L F H P X
M F E C N O A R M L N N E E E
C N J E R U T N E V D A A T L
S I I O N U M N N M K S V B P
E R Y T B O G U T S A N E D M
F W S O R E M B R A C I N G O
P L A Y I N G D Y D N A H S C
```

Adventure	Excitement	Life
Americano	Family	Money
Aunts	Friends	Musicians
Challenge	Gerlando	Newspapers
Chops	Handy	Playing
Compilati	Heaven	Practice
Complex	Inferiority	Skills
Cousins	Italy	Speaks
Drum	Job	Thrill
Embracing	Joy	Uncles

Curiosity

Many of us are uncertain about our place in the world. It's a vast and complex place. We can easily feel lost. We pass by so many people every day. We find ourselves in so many places. Sometimes this may make us think that we are far too small. Or perhaps we feel as though we do not know enough. Or we are somehow not enough.

Remember that we each have a valuable place on this planet that is uniquely our own. We are both infinite and infinitesimal. The world around us is wondrous and wide, and so is the world inside of us. Find joy in this balance.

Know you are important on this planet. Stay curious and kind. Life is for exploration. Do not put too much pressure on yourself. We are not meant to understand everything.

We begin to understand our place when we accept that we are always changing. It is amazing that we are able to be part of such a beautiful collection of experiences. There is so much out there to learn and feel. Allow yourself to experiment and explore. Our place in this world may be unclear sometimes. Embrace that uncertainty. It's the human thing to do.

—*Dahlia Suiter*

Inspired Wisdom:

___ ____ __ _____ ___

_____ __ ____ _____

____ _____ ____

_____

```
A P L A C E C R D A H L I A W
L E S U O R E D N O W A T E I
L S A E H U M A N W P L A C D
O E U F C U O L E R O L P X E
W R Y I F N O U U R T R E S C
C E L E T C E F L F E C L O I
E H E X P E R I M E N T M D N
T L A T T R R T R A A P H Y V
I I S N W T S U L E L R T O A
N R L A G A P A E E P I N M L
I D T T V I B E X C S X A H U
F A T R R N N B C O A Z E D A
N E Y O J T F G I C I R N L B
I E C P T Y S R Y N A I B O L
U R A M W E U S G O K M E M E
N N O I T C E L L O C E S S E
```

Accept	Embrace	Learn
Allow	Experiences	Place
Amazing	Experiment	Planet
Balance	Explore	Suiter
Beautiful	Feel	Uncertainty
Changing	Human	Valuable
Collection	Important	Vast
Complex	Infinite	Wide
Curiosity	Joy	Wonderous
Dahlia	Kind	World

The Reach

I think our choices bring us our most important lessons as we navigate our way through life. Some are good and some are bad. The end result is that we made it through.

Of the many trips I have taken, some 250,000 miles at sea, making it safe for the vessel and crew was my primary mission. I have patterned my life around this saying: *Life is a reach. However, do not reach into a storm.*

Reach denotes many things in life in this context. Sail with the wind at your beam. Extend your horizons. Go to sea not knowing what is ahead yet have the courage to complete the voyage.

Reaching into a storm is something entirely different. It means being cautious when there is the possibility of danger ahead. Turn around to live another day. Sometimes we can't get there from here even if we want to. Mother Nature is the determining factor in these life-and-death decisions. Many sailors have perished because they did not or could not take heed of the dangers ahead, change direction, and seek safe harbor.

There is no better feeling than when you have made it out of danger and to safety. I look back at all the times I chose to turn around and lost ground in the direction I was headed. It didn't feel good at the time. Now I am grateful to be here to sail on another day. Fair winds and blue skies are the reward for surviving the storms.

—*Captain Dennis Daoust*

Inspired Wisdom:

_ _

_ _

_ _ _ _

```
S S E C I O H C O M S D N I W
E R A T I N M T D E N N I S S
V E S S E L I N S E M B S A E
S A D E R U T A N U L A I Y G
H C O I U M R V T U O L E N A
O H A R R E T I E P O A O B R
R H L O E E S G A R A I D H U
I S T E G A C A S F S C A I O
Z S K A S S L T A S N R H R C
O D Y I A S S E I O B E E E M
N O E F E T O M I O M H E G E
V S E Y O S U N R A N T D N R
E C A U T I O U S T H O E A W
C R E W I D R A W E R M N D D
```

Beam	Direction	Reach
Blue	Fair	Reward
Captain	Harbor	Safe
Cautious	Heed	Sailors
Choices	Horizon	Sea
Courage	Lessons	Skies
Crew	Mission	Storm
Danger	Mother	Vessel
Daoust	Nature	Voyage
Dennis	Navigate	Winds

Wisdom of the Inner Child

We all experience challenges in life. During these times it can be easy to forget about laughter, joy, and connection. We might even feel separate from others and from ourselves.

What if we believed that everything is happening for us, rather than to us? This might even mean that our path is always illuminated. We can use curiosity to come home to ourselves. When we return to our *heartspace*, we tap into a part of us that is wise, loving, and compassionate. This is a special place where our inner child resides.

The soul of a child is magic. It can be joyous to hear the laughter of youth. There can be such sweetness in simple things. Humans often seek outside sources of happiness, forgetting all that lives within.

We can catch a glimpse of our inner child in simple, unplanned moments. Maybe we find ourselves humming a song, or smiling because the sun is shining. When there is no self-judgment, and lots of compassion, we are free to be. We can give ourselves the gift of permission to be present and honor all of who we are. This opens us up to more lightness of being and bliss. This wisdom is the pureness of our innocence. It is a wonderful space to place our trust.

Remember something joyful from your childhood. Playing in the sprinklers on a hot summer day, eating popsicles, laughing so hard your face hurts, the cool rain on your face, or splashing in puddles. Let that joy fill, refresh, and renew you from head to toe. Celebrate your inner child today.

—*Maura A. Finn*

Inspired Wisdom:

_ _

_ _

_ _

_ _ _ _ _ _

```
W E N E R R B L I S S S E M F
E M B P U D D L E S P W E A R
A N D L E T A R B E L E C O V
T R U S T E F Y O N A E O U R
I S P O P S I C L E S T M N N
E S A U C I N N E R H N P R C
H E R L H M N I Y U I E A L D
T N U E I O O C T P N S S F H
H T A I L N C D I D G S S A S
U H M J D K E L S G L S I T E
M G H O H E N J O I A I O O R
M I Y Y O T C I I H W M N A F
I L T F O H E A R T S P A C E
N Y O U D U S E U P E L T K R
G N I L I M S W C I S E E T H
I G N I V O L A U G H I N G N
```

Bliss	Innocence	Refresh
Celebrate	Joyful	Renew
Childhood	Laughing	Simple
Compassionate	Lightness	Smiling
Curiosity	Loving	Soul
Face	Magic	Splashing
Finn	Maura	Sprinklers
Heartspace	Popsicles	Sweetness
Humming	Puddles	Trust
Inner	Pureness	Wisdom

The Power of Play

When was the last time you played and had fun?

We don't stop playing because we get old; we get old because we stop playing.
—George Bernard Shaw

Play. It's as natural and necessary as sleep, touch, and companionship. Play. It's as pervasive as children, laughter, and family. Play. It's as accessible as water, light, and soil. Play. It's a great and humble activity that springs from our species like fruit from trees.

Play is not just for children. It's a lifelong ingredient in a well-lived life. It's a great way to fuel imagination, creativity, and emotional wellness. Giving ourselves permission to play can boost our energy and vitality plus improve resistance to disease, helping us function at our best.

Play reduces stress, fosters learning, and promotes problem-solving. Every indigenous culture throughout time has encouraged hours of play each day. The developing field of brain research affirms the wisdom of this in study after study. It proves that play has a powerful and positive effect on the brain's structure and function, enhancing brain growth in the young and even creating new brain cells in the mature and in victims of debilitating head traumas.

On a social level, the simple act of playing improves self-management, social awareness, relationship skills, and personal and group decision-making.

Know someone who is miserable and at odds with themselves and those around them? Ask this simple question: "How much do you play?" The answer is almost always "Not enough." At that point, it's our honor as loving humans to reach out our hands and offer, "Then let's go play."

—*Izzi Tooinsky*

Inspired Wisdom:

‐‐‐‐‐‐‐‐‐‐ ‐‐‐‐ ‐‐‐‐ ‐‐‐‐‐‐‐
‐‐‐‐ ‐‐‐‐‐‐‐ ‐‐‐‐‐ ‐‐‐‐ ‐‐‐‐‐‐
‐‐ ‐‐‐‐‐‐‐‐‐ ‐‐‐‐

```
I  T  I  U  R  F  N  C  R  E  R  E  T  A  W
L  I  G  H  T  A  L  A  U  G  H  T  E  R  S
M  H  C  U  O  T  G  S  H  S  I  E  J  P  O
A  Y  A  N  O  N  D  N  E  U  H  Z  E  E  C
T  B  R  A  I  N  A  E  I  O  M  C  Z  M  R
U  L  T  V  N  N  R  H  C  N  I  B  O  I  E
R  A  L  N  S  T  G  H  D  E  R  D  L  W  A
E  O  L  F  K  O  I  R  S  G  S  A  S  E  T
S  N  U  D  Y  L  E  L  E  I  R  S  E  W  I
S  N  F  I  D  L  I  T  W  D  E  H  T  L  V
L  L  R  R  N  O  I  T  A  N  I  G  A  M  I
L  H  E  E  S  P  O  M  L  I  W  E  E  R  T
E  N  W  E  Y  T  I  L  A  T  I  V  N  O  Y
C  F  O  P  P  O  E  S  I  F  T  I  V  T  E
P  L  P  A  Y  W  E  N  E  R  G  Y  A  L  P
```

Brain	Indigenous	Soil
Cells	Ingredient	Solving
Children	Izzi	Species
Creativity	Laughter	Tooinsky
Energy	Learning	Touch
Family	Light	Trees
Fruit	Mature	Vitality
Fun	Play	Water
Humble	Powerful	Wellness
Imagination	Sleep	Wisdom

9 Laugh, Dance, Sing, Play!

Remember when you didn't care what someone thought of you? For most of us, it is a distant childhood memory. What were you doing? Do you recall that when you were a child you did what you wanted to do? At least sometimes? Children often don't hesitate for a moment to do what brings them joy. Often loud, it is a screaming, laughing, giggling, exuberant joy. Today, we call it impulsive. When we were children, it was called having fun. Or just playing.

The fear of judgement didn't even cross our minds. We sang at the top of our lungs. We dressed up and went out in public in a tutu, favorite princess dress, pirate, or ninja costume. We played like horses in the yard and galloped with complete abandon. We had tea parties with real mud pies. We flipped over rocks and picked up lizards without fearing we'd catch a disease. Bugs were cool or icky or tasty!

We explored the world, with eyes and imaginations wide open. We let our curiosity lead. We followed our whims. Joy and play and sunshine were all the fuel we needed. Those were wonderful, magical experiences. Being free and having fun was the goal. Remember what it was like?

Go out and do something today that allows your inner child's curiosity to live in full expression. Run through the grass barefoot. Dance without caring who's watching. Build a pillow fort. Laugh out loud. And always, always take a moment to sing. At the top of your lungs. Experience and enjoy life to its fullest. You can do it. You already know how. You learned as a child. Remember.

—*Anna Pereira*

Inspired Wisdom:

__ _____ _____ __ ____

___ ___ ___

_____ _ _____

____ _____

```
I A L P B F L S S D R A Z I L
S P L I O A I A P I E S P T O
U W L R M N R G U S Y E N U S
N E T A G L N E G G R F O T T
S M O T Y I F N F E H E I U S
H E A E L C U R I O S I T Y S
I B U G S L L R T H O E A J E
N O G Y I A A N E E D T N E C
E I P N T C H U E B S I I A N
G N I N J A A R Y S M A G M I
E I L D R E F L M R N E A E R
C M L L U F R E D N O W M B P
N E O R F M R O A M C M I E H
A I W P A R T I E S L D E H R
D S M I H W O O S K C O R M D
```

Anna	Lizards	Pirate
Barefoot	Lungs	Play
Bugs	Magical	Princess
Curiosity	Memory	Remember
Dance	Mud	Rocks
Fort	Ninja	Sing
Free	Parties	Sunshine
Giggling	Pereira	Tutu
Imagination	Pies	Whims
Laugh	Pillow	Wonderful

Inspiration

I am so happy to be alive to enjoy this day! I am fortunate to live an inspired life, full of joy and gratitude and feeling blessed. This wonderful feeling is something I have cultivated over time. Eighty years, to be precise. I have learned that I can choose to feel this way, and it feels great!

I discovered a secret long ago. I learned that we can be inspired by gratitude to feel happy and blessed. Daily doses of inspiration create a great amount of joy in our lives.

Beginning each day feeling grateful starts things on a positive note. You can become inspired by the littlest things. I am inspired by the sun shining through my bedroom window. By the wildflowers in a vase on my breakfast table. By finding the perfect parking space. This feeling of gratitude puts me in a wonderful mood. It is an attitude to cultivate.

No matter how insignificant they may seem, we are surrounded by things to be grateful for. The taste of a juicy peach. A butterfly flitting by. The thoughtfulness of a friend. An even number of socks from the dryer. Our lives are filled with so many inspiring moments. Once we start looking for them, we will begin to see them everywhere.

Become aware of your many blessings. Count them like little sheep when you wake up and when you go to sleep. Create a more joy-filled life. We are all so truly blessed!

—*Geraldine Gehrke Schwartz*

Inspired Wisdom:

__ _____ ____ ___ ____ ___
____ __ _____ _____
___ ___ ____ _____

```
P  P  E  E  H  S  W  E  A  S  L  E  E  P  B
G  O  S  E  C  R  E  T  R  E  S  E  S  O  D
R  S  S  I  W  N  T  G  D  M  K  O  C  R  E
A  K  J  I  O  I  Y  N  E  R  D  A  H  I  N
T  C  T  O  T  O  L  N  U  N  Y  U  W  R  E
I  O  L  U  I  I  I  D  E  O  F  E  A  E  K
T  S  D  B  Y  D  V  I  F  I  C  E  R  E  R
U  E  L  Y  L  F  R  E  T  T  U  B  T  I  H
D  N  D  A  G  F  G  R  S  A  A  T  Z  T  E
E  A  R  E  W  O  N  D  E  R  F  U  L  A  G
I  E  W  T  S  M  U  D  E  I  E  F  O  S  R
G  O  U  A  O  S  H  A  P  P  Y  W  R  T  L
N  M  O  O  R  D  E  B  M  S  A  N  O  E  E
U  Y  D  B  L  E  E  L  E  N  J  O  Y  L  E
S  S  H  C  A  E  P  S  B  I  I  N  G  S  F
```

Attitude	Flowers	Schwartz
Aware	Friend	Secret
Bedroom	Gehrke	Sheep
Blessed	Geraldine	Sleep
Butterfly	Gratitude	Socks
Count	Happy	Sun
Doses	Inspiration	Taste
Dryer	Mood	Wake
Enjoy	Peach	Wild
Feel	Positive	Wonderful

How to Get Inspired

What inspires you? What fills your being to the brim with endless enthusiasm? What permeates your body, mind, heart, and spirit with a sense of fulfillment, purpose, and curiosity in every waking moment? What makes you feel like you are walking on air with a smile on your face? Why, it's almost like being in love.

Historically, inspiration referred to how a supernatural being uses a person as an instrument for the delivery of Divine or previously unknown truths. Sacred teachings worldwide over the millennia were inspired, transmitted, downloaded, and communicated to humanity through messengers like Moses, Lao-Tzu, Muhammad, and Gautama Buddha. A muse whispers knowledge into the ears of scientists, poets, and artists. Many of our world-changing inventions, masterpieces, and discoveries have arrived fully formed in the consciousness of the creator unbidden from beyond the beyond.

Inspiration is a key motivator of creativity. We are inspired from within and without. What fuels inspiration? Illumination, nature, beauty, and goodness are some of the most commonly reported triggers.

Over the past decade, scientists and researchers have tested and found strong support that inspiration is both a trait and a state that seems to vary both between and within individuals.* Inspiration compels us to bring ideas into existence. It has the power to effect change not just for the one, but also for the many. It facilitates progress toward goals and increases well-being through giving us a sense of purpose.

*Published on the U.S. Department of Health and Human Services' National Center for Biotechnology Information website.

A moment of clarity that is often vivid, inspiration is an "aha" moment that can take the form of a grand vision, or a seeing of something one has not seen before, even if it was always there. Time perception often shifts from tick-tock clock time to a time-dilation stretch when a moment seems like an eternity. Inspiration involves both being inspired *by* something *and acting on* that inspiration.

Inspired people share certain characteristics. Researchers Todd M. Thrash and Andrew J. Elliot developed an *Inspiration Scale* which measures the frequency with which a person experiences inspiration in their daily lives. They found that the most-often-inspired were more open to new experiences, as well as more absorbed in their tasks.

Inspired people also expressed higher levels of important psychological resources, including belief in their own abilities, self-esteem, and optimism. Mastery and love of work, engagement, creativity, perceived competence, self-esteem, and optimism were all consequences of inspiration. Interestingly, work mastery also often came before inspiration, which suggests that inspiration is not purely passive and favors the prepared mind.

We can fertilize our inspirations and make them real on the physical plane. Many of us have great ideas. How do we bring them to physical reality? Here are some possible practical steps to take if inspiration calls loudly and insistently. If now is not the moment, keep them in mind for the future, just in case.

Inspiration is fertilized with intention. That intention is the human version of the potency of the birds and the bees and the butterflies that pollinates a flower to fruition. When your goal is to make your vision a reality, you pollinate it with intention.

One of the best ways to fertilize an inspiration is by writing it down. Sometimes a new dedicated notebook is just the thing. Now the inspiration knows that the intention is there for it to manifest because it now has a landing spot in this world: the notebook. That begins the grounding process. Use that book for any ideas and images that surface. Once the idea is written down and has a place to grow, it starts to take on a life of its own.

The next step is to plan how to accomplish this vision. What will you do? How can you make it happen? How will it feel when you see it complete? Don't worry if you don't know the details of every single step. Those will come. Experiment to find out what works and what doesn't.

There are many effective goal-achievement techniques out there. They all say you need to see and acknowledge the vision as real and feel the energy of achieving the fullness of your dream. Many use affirmations and creative visualizations for these steps. Others like vision boards or other art pieces to help the process along. Some people are planners, with charts and graphs. Use what works for you.

After the energetic phase has been activated, it is time to take action. You can do whatever you set out to do if you break it down into achievable steps. Do something every day toward making your vision a reality, no matter how small it may seem. The days will add up, until one day your notebook will be full. Before you know it, you will have the profound pleasure of seeing your dream right before your eyes. This is one of the most beautiful sights there is to behold. It's a dream come true. When this magical moment happens, savor it.

Whether your dream is a small herb garden or a worldwide business, consider planting the seeds of your inspirations today. Even if only in your heart. Give yourself permission to dream. To imagine. Consider all the negatives of your past as very rich and growth-filled, fragrant fertilizer. Wisdom really can come at any age. Youth has enthusiasm that can spark ideas. Age has experience that can guide and facilitate. It's not too late. You're not too old, or too young, or too broke, or too busy, or too tired, or too fat, or too thin, or too anything else.

Let your rich dreams inspire you.

Let your visions be considered at least possible, if not inevitable.

Let yourself live an inspired life.

Why not?

Love Your Neighbor and Yourself

Do you have dreams? Want to save the world? Or even just live peacefully with those around you?

We all know the saying "Love your neighbor as you love yourself." It's the "as you love yourself" part that we often miss. It rather sadly seems that most of us are doing an excellent job of loving our neighbors just as poorly as we love ourselves.

Think about it. If you don't accept yourself, how can you possibly fully accept another? If you are not relentlessly kind to yourself, where do you get the inspiration, energy, and stamina to be endlessly kind to others? If taking care of others comes first, where does that put you? Second, third-place, last?

Yet we can love our neighbors and ourselves. Here's the blueprint. Start by going into your heart and searching for the love there. Feel it. Then hold onto it. Persistently. Bring that feeling of love to the surface all throughout the day. Infuse that love into an everyday object like a coffee mug, a ring, a water bottle, whatever works for you, to anchor that feeling as a visual reminder. Then when something is scary, challenging, or overwhelming, touch that object and feel the love. It will calm you and remind you to flow love into your thoughts and actions. Love is within you, yours for the asking.

Love your neighbor by loving yourself, and you will save the world. Lovingly do deep, soul-searching work on yourself, and, in fact, you already have.

—*Bertha Edington*

Inspired Wisdom:

— —————— ——— —————— ————— ———

—— ————— ———— ———

—————— —— ——————

```
E R I S O B J E C T E N P C H
A V E N T V W M N G V E E E E
T H A L O H I A L E O I A L W
O R L S E I G S T A L G C T R
C D E S A N T U U E C H E T I
C O O H D Y T A O A R B F O N
A U F Y R T L L R H L O U B G
L S B F P E A S E I T R L Y B
T E M E E H M E S S P I L N G
K O C A T E D I A E S S Y I R
N C U R E I D A N N L L N N O
A D E C N R L O V D I D Y I H
I B N G H G D T O M E M N Y C
S E T Y O U R S E L F R A E N
L O A C T I O N S C A R E T A
N F Y G R E N E E S U F N I S
```

Accept	Endlessly	Ring
Actions	Energy	Save
Anchor	Infuse	Soul
Bertha	Inspiration	Stamina
Bottle	Love	Thoughts
Calm	Neighbor	Touch
Care	Object	Visual
Coffee	Peacefully	Water
Dreams	Relentlessly	Yourself
Edington	Reminder	

Simple Truths to Practice

Stretch your comfort zone. Be amazed by what you learn and experience. Stay open-minded.

Practice positive self-talk. Appreciate your accomplishments and be a helpful friend to yourself.

Respect your body. It will last a lifetime. Be attentive and take good care of it.

Don't take things personally. Everyone has their own stuff going on, so let other people's issues go.

Connect with the Divine and trust your intuition. There is something bigger than each of us which guides and supports us. We see it in synchronicities, auspicious signs, animal sightings, vivid dreams, messages from songs, and other "aha" moments. Watch and pay attention.

Celebrate and be grateful. Appreciate the little, special moments, and know there is purpose in all life experiences.

Be disciplined and prepared. Plan ahead, have goals, stay organized. Practice and develop skills before you need them.

Appreciate others. The more we value others and genuinely wish them well, the happier and more fulfilled we are. Great relationships bring joy to all. Don't compare. Be kind.

Be useful. Give back. Having a purpose makes life meaningful and rewarding.

Admit mistakes. This is surprisingly powerful and often difficult to do. Acknowledge to yourself and others when you mess up. Apologize and make amends.

Accept impermanence. Everything changes, so be flexible. Adapt and bounce back from frustrations and upsets. How we respond to adversity makes all the difference!

—*Maryann Sperry*

Inspired Wisdom:

___ ___ ___   ___ ___ ___ ___ ___ ___ ___ ___   ___ ___ ___ ___ ___ ___ ___

___ ___ ___   ___ ___ ___ ___   ___   ___ ___ ___ ___ ___   ___ ___ ___ ___

```
E C E L E B R A T E C N U O B
N E T H E T A I C E R P P A E
I U N N V E L B I X E L F I V
V E M I S T A K E S T I M D A
I Y V R L N N A Y R A M R P S
D I D S E P U R P O S E O N I
D S U O I C I P S U A L E A G
A D C L B N T C H M O P M U H
S C E O U O T U S G O A T S T
G T C R N F H U I I Z T P E I
Y O R E A N E Z I E D U A F N
W E R E P P E T D T E A D U G
T R U S T T E C A N I M A L S
R E S P E C T R T R G O R E A
S P E R R Y H T P I G D N E A
```

Accept	Celebrate	Open
Adapt	Connect	Prepared
Admit	Discipline	Purpose
Amazed	Divine	Respect
Animal	Dreams	Sightings
Apologize	Flexible	Sperry
Appreciate	Grateful	Stretch
Auspicious	Intuition	Trust
Body	Maryann	Useful
Bounce	Mistakes	Vivid

13 Cultivate Inner Peace

Come on a journey. Sit quietly. Close your eyes. Imagine being at the river. You are sitting on a rock in the early-morning sun at a beautiful swimming hole. The pool of water is flowing so calmly that the rocks, the trees, and the sky reflect a perfect mirror image. You are surrounded by beauty. Drink it in. Let the tranquility refresh your spirit. Relax and breathe.

This sublime scene describes the consciousness, which is reflected in a peaceful, centered mind. In Hindu philosophy, this is called *sattva*. The mind is a calm pool, with no agitation or ripples of thoughts and feelings. Who wouldn't want to attain this state of being on a daily basis? Or enjoy dipping a toe into it to clear your inner slate throughout a busy day? Let the ripples melt away.

Sattva is a reflection of the evolution of our soul's journey. We travel from ignorance to awareness, then into transcendence. We can take conscious steps from the moment we wake up to when we close our eyes at night to cultivate this inner peace.

Eating fresh food, meditation, allowing space in relationships, clean surroundings, and time in nature all nurture *sattva*. This lifestyle helps place us into our serene center, the present moment.

It's a worthy practice, especially when we are not able to physically be at our sacred river pool. Yet our minds and hearts can take us there in an instant. Let's go there together right now. Inhale. Exhale. Ahhh....

—*Kim Kinjo*

Inspired Wisdom:

_ _ _ _ _   _ _ _ _   _ _ _ _ _ _ _ _   _ _
_ _ _ _   _ _ _ _ _ _   _ _   _ _   _ _ _ _ _ _ _
_ _ _   _ _ _ _ _ _ _

```
B T R A N Q U I L I T Y R I S
N R E V I R G Y O X A L E R E
U M G N A T U R E H L R A W R
A I S N R S E W S N U T N E E
S K U S I T A E O N F O L O N
H E B R Y P R T U R I O U E E
E R L B I F P R T T T R E E M
A A I A E P T I A V U H C L W
R T M R H U P T D L A L Y A H
T O E T R X I L O O E B T H M
S J E E C D E O E A B E E N I
N N T E E R P E N S R D A I N
N I D M E T A V I T L U C P D
R K R E N N I E S P E A C E S
S A C R E D E Y L M L A C N T
```

Beautiful	Kinjo	Ripples
Calmly	Meditation	River
Clean	Melt	Sacred
Cultivate	Minds	Sattva
Dipping	Nature	Serene
Exhale	Nurture	Sublime
Hearts	Peace	Tranquility
Inhale	Pool	Water
Inner	Refresh	Worthy
Kim	Relax	

The Mystery in Silence

What surrounds us? What do we interact with that we may not be aware of? We walk through our lives day by day moving through thoughts, feelings, energy patterns, and many more forms of unseen influences. It's easy to recognize emotions directed toward us from other people, and usually difficult to ignore our own thoughts.

But how about those invisible energy patterns that exist in the world around us?

There are environments that make us feel connected to our Source and those that help us feel creatively inspired. For instance, the energy in temples and churches, museums and libraries, and natural settings like forests, deserts, beaches, and mountaintops. Each has a different, noticeable effect on us.

We can't see it, but we can sure feel it, especially when we know how to quiet our own thoughts and feelings. This is a learned skill developed through things like meditation and time spent in quiet environments without any connection to the noise of civilization.

How do we find time for silence in this busy world? Perhaps a cup of coffee on the back porch early in the morning or a walk in the park after a long day. The opportunities are there and are often found in the places that inspire us or connect us to the natural world.

Listen to the sounds of silence and connect deeply within yourself. Immerse yourself in the profoundly mystical power of the invisible world.

—Ingrid Coffin

Inspired Wisdom:

—— ——— —————— ——— ——————

——— —— ———— ——— ———— —— ——

——— —————

```
J S U S N R E T T A P S T B N
S K E C S S A U S O U R C E A
E I N I A T N U O M T F M S T
H L E C Y N R O U C U E C A U
C L L O N E N E E O D E E T R
A S A F E M E N S I I L S E A
E T C F D N N S T E B I C U L
B O I I O O E A T I D N E C M
S N T N C R T M S H E G O H Q
S T S M E I E I O L G S A U K
E N Y I O V V S I T A U I R L
L T M N I N S S T W I E O C A
P A R K I E N O A S T O T H W
M T L I B R A R I E S H N E T
E Y G R E N E E P O R C H S R
T E I M M E R S E D I R G N I
```

Aware	Forests	Park
Beaches	Immerse	Patterns
Churches	Ingrid	Porch
Coffin	Invisible	Quiet
Connect	Libraries	Silence
Deserts	Meditation	Skill
Emotions	Mountain	Source
Energy	Museums	Temples
Environments	Mystical	Thoughts
Feelings	Natural	Walk

Life Skills 101

How do we develop important life skills? Things like discipline, integrity, and confidence? What about self-control? We all see the value in these things, but how do we grow them? In our lives? In our inner sanctums? How do we stretch our individual capacities?

My teachers encouraged me to seek, to strive for, discipline, integrity, and confidence. How does one build such things?

After years of training and searching, I've found a simple answer: memory. Deep memory. Tribal memory. At least for me, the answers lie there. When we remember, we can hone our skills. We embrace integrity to achieve. We hold ourselves accountable. We develop the discipline to keep doing it every time we remember.

Of course, sometimes we forget, which is okay. That's how we learn. This works. That doesn't. This grows me in a direction I want. That doesn't feel so good. What we choose to do when we remember is key.

When I can master a skill and remember to employ it ten out of ten times, I build confidence. In the study of kung fu, I strive to master a craft. That craft transfers into daily life and everyday activities. It changes how I sweep the floor or make the bed. If I wanted to become a doctor, it would change the way I did that, too. With discipline and integrity, I create more success than failure. This builds confidence.

Daily application and consistent practice are what develop discipline. Activities become habitual. Careful choice cultivates integrity. With both discipline and integrity, confidence soars. How do we build life skills? One choice at a time.

—*Nick DeVincenzo*

Inspired Wisdom:

_ _ _ _   _ _ _ _ _ _ _

_ _ _ _ _ _ _ _ _ _ _ _ _   _ _ _   _ _   _ _

_ _ _ _   _ _   _ _ _ _ _ _   _ _ _ _ _ _

_ _ _ _ _   _ _ _

```
I L O Z N E C N I V E D I F E
N S T R I V E C V A L U E R M
N R E A S Y T I R G E T N I A
E E N O H M T E S O F P P O S
R H A C C O U N T A B L E R T
T C U P O N T R R A I D T E
I A E O E S N C C U I I S M R
F E O N E E R S D N S B P M E
L T T F D I C I I C A L A O A
E K C I N T V I I S O S G L C
A Y Y D R I O P T Y T E W M H
R R Y E D V L S U C C E S S I
N O C N K I H O S I A E N N E
S M I C N T G R O W K R I T V
L E L E S C E H S W E E P V E
E M R Y D A C A Y U F G N U K
```

Accountable	Employ	Memory
Achieve	Grow	Nick
Activities	Hone	Practice
Choice	Individual	Sanctums
Confidence	Inner	Strive
Consistent	Integrity	Success
Craft	Key	Sweep
Deep	Kung Fu	Teachers
DeVincenzo	Learn	Tribal
Discipline	Master	Value

It's Your Choice

Life decisions can be like flipping a coin. It's not a gamble. It's a reminder that there are at least two responses to every situation. We can get exhausted considering the pluses and minuses of every option. Or we can become invigorated. How we react to life's constant choices can leave us feeling depressed and floundering or positive and self-assured.

The little things, like what kind of toast we prefer—white, wheat, rye, or gluten-free—may not be huge. Recognizing that we have a choice is. Not every choice is simple. Some require meditation, prayer, consultation with those we trust, or deep thought. By making them intentionally, we feel empowered. Choosing a healthy response to the small things can get us through those tough times that feel like a punch in the gut. We've set up a positive response mechanism.

Today, consider the things you say and do as choices. What if a car cuts you off on the freeway? You can get mad, honk, and yell. Or you can decide that they must be in a big hurry, and let them go by like a cloud in the sky. Getting angry may feel appropriate at the moment, but that feeling can turn into internal brooding and a grey spirit. Smiling at them says that you don't care. This isn't worth messing my day up over.

By choosing happy over sad or mad, we set ourselves up for a more positive life. Heads or tails? It's your call!

—*Jayne Sams*

Inspired Wisdom:

— ————— ——————————

—————————————— ——— —————— ——

—— —— ——————————

——————

Cristina Smith & Rick Smith

```
I M H E A L T H Y A T A E H W
K E E T I H W H D E C P I S I
G P O S I E M P O W E R E D N
N S O C N O N S S U C N U E P
I I S S V O O U I S G O Y R D
P L E Y I A P N D N L H A A C
P H S O G T O S O C A Y T M J
I G U L O S I I E T E H I F E
L T L O R T T V B R E N C R A
F A P U A A N O E U U I P E S
C N O I T A T L U S N O C E M
T I L I E E M I E T S C T W A
I S D C D P N S H A P P Y A S
E E C I O H C H E A D S R Y S
M T O A S T G N I L I M S O N
```

Call	Happy	Prayer
Choice	Heads	Response
Cloud	Healthy	Sams
Coin	Invigorated	Smiling
Consultation	Jayne	Tails
Deep	Mechanism	Thought
Empowered	Meditation	Toast
Flipping	Minuses	Trust
Freeway	Pluses	Wheat
Gluten	Positive	White

Healing Happy

I live with chronic illness.

In coping with that, I've learned how to change my fixed mindset to a positive one. It has made me realize that my body and symptoms may not always be controllable, but my mindset is. This is how I manage, despite the pain day in and day out.

Healing has its good days and bad days, but we can choose to focus on the positive. Energy flows where attention goes.

I've learned to do what I call "healing happy." Healing happy means enjoying the journey regardless of the process the body is going through.

For my own treatment, I've chosen holistic healing. It heals the body, mind, and spirit. My approach includes a natural lifestyle and diet, homeopathic remedies, essential oils, vitamins, and supplements. Pain and stress-relieving therapies consist of acupressure, cupping, infrared sauna, massage, and more. I strive for a healthy mindset by practicing daily affirmations, energy medicine, guided meditation and visualizations, hypnotherapy, and yin/restorative yoga.

I practice self-care at home as well as with professionals. Self-care is giving ourselves the very best so that we aren't just settling with what is left after pouring out our life force to others. Self-care is a form of love.

Nobody is responsible for loving us but ourselves. We have the opportunity to express that love better than anyone else possibly could. Why not do so in full?

It is my wish that you enjoy and may benefit from a few of the things that help me. Heal and be happy. I wish all a life filled with joy.

—*Brittany Lee*

Inspired Wisdom:

— — — — — — —   — — —   — — — — — — — —

— — — — — —   — — —   — — — — — — —   — —

— — — —   — —   — — —   — — — — — — — — — — — —

```
T M H O T E S D N I M S Y O J
U A R Y O G A Y G H Y T Y H B
S S A E G A N A M M C N E D E
E S Y A S A T S P T I A N T N
C A U I T T D T N E L C R O E
R G N T N T O R F I O L U E F
O E I C O M U R N O M R O Q I
F R U U S T A G A L C A J I T
B T Y P O F E L T T I U T C F
S Y E P H O L I S T I C S I I
A G N I A E R L D L C V I N V
U R R N C I V Y P P A H E O L
N E U G P P R O C E S S M R E
A N S S T A N C L Y D O B H E
E E V I T I S O P L I F E C S
```

Benefit	Happy	Mindset
Body	Healing	Positive
Brittany	Holistic	Process
Care	Journey	Restorative
Chronic	Joy	Sauna
Cupping	Lee	Spirit
Diet	Life	Symptoms
Energy	Love	Vitamins
Focus	Manage	Yin
Force	Massage	Yoga

Hope

Hope inspires. It keeps us going in dark times and boosts us higher in good times. Hope is a feeling of expectation and desire for a certain thing to happen. It encompasses an optimistic state of mind. Hope is not necessarily based on facts or what may be going on in our lives. It is a feeling, rising from intuition or a sense in the gut, that there is a positive outcome at the end.

Sometimes we hope that someone we love will turn their life around. Or we hope the world will mellow out and peace will prevail on Earth. Or we hope to find someone special to love and care for us. Whatever it is, hope supports us in our human endeavors. It is something to be embraced, maintained, and nurtured.

Sometimes our hopes require action. We can contribute our energy to make our hopes more likely to come to fruition. Hope is not a strategy. This well-known saying tells us that it's not enough to just hope things will happen. We need to do what we can to help make it happen. It is our thoughts, words, and actions that really get us where we want to go.

Cultivating and fostering our hope supports our personal, professional, and spiritual growth. Why? Because hope is one of the catalysts that grow the roots and foundations of our very being. Without hope there is no power. Let it emerge and inspire. Be powerful. Be hopeful. Rise to your own occasion.

—*Darity Wesley*

Inspired Wisdom:

__ ____ _____ __ __ __
_____ ___ _____ __
_____ ____ ___
_____ _____

```
M P Y G E T A R T S T S O O B
Y O C E M E R G E H T N O P E
P W A P B L I M E L L O W F T
S E T O R S O C C A S I O N M
T R A H A E U M O P N T T R O
H S L C C U I S N T O C A I N
G E Y D E N I A T N I A M A N
U D S C D G N I R E T S O F A
O P T I M I S T I C A R W R R
H Y S D R O W Y B M D E E U T
T H T N O I T I U T N I S I R
O G N I T A V I T L U C L T U
G H N U R T U R E D O E E I V
E N T H E A T O U G F V Y O H
E S T T I M D E S Y G R E N E
```

Actions	Foundations	Optimistic
Boosts	Fruition	Peace
Catalysts	Hope	Power
Contribute	Intuition	Rise
Cultivating	Love	Roots
Darity	Maintained	Strategy
Embraced	Mellow	Thoughts
Emerge	Mind	Wesley
Energy	Nurtured	Words
Fostering	Occasion	

Walk Your True Path

Are your steps into your future clear? We are each on our own path. We can only be on one path at a time. We are called to remember ourselves as individuals and distinct parts of the glorious whole of the Universe. As we do this, our brilliant uniqueness shows up to shine its light on the world. Cherish your exceptionally special light. It is as radiant and sparkly as the stars that illuminate the heavens. Our inner understandings enlighten ourselves and others.

Some of our ancient wisdom down here, below the stars, comes from myths, stories, and archetypes from the skies above. We are never truly lost nor are we ever actually alone. Our own mysterious inner wisdom has been guiding us since birth or maybe even before from our ancestral and karmic lineage. It never leaves us.

To cultivate your exquisite wisdom, remember to hold and care for yourself as one would a precious newborn babe. It helps to slow down, and to stop doing so much. Simply be alone with that individual inner light that is the real you. Hold this light up like a lantern and embrace your authentic self. Offer to light the way for others in your own singularly exceptional way. Walking your true path takes constant courage on the journey to genuine freedom.

—*Shelley Hines*

Inspired Wisdom:

__ __ ___ ____ __ __ __

__ _____ ____ __ ____ __ __

___ ___ _____

```
M T S O I R B Y E L T E H E E
R O E U E N E L A A X U N L M
E I D F O L D R A C N L S R T
O B F S L I T I E I I E E T S
L O R E I S R P V G C N U R E
L A H Y E W T E H I N E A F N
R S N C H I R T T I D T P S I
E E N T O S E A C S S U U S U
E A A N E N T N S N Y O A O N
G P A E S R L I I N I M V L E
A L E W H T N M I R E T N P G
R W E B T R A U O C E V S A N
U A D O Y U H L B A B E A I A
O L R R M E G L H I N E S E D
C K M N S U O I C E R P O N H
S P A R K L Y A N C I E N T Y
```

Ancestral	Hines	Precious
Ancient	Illuminate	Shelley
Babe	Individual	Sparkly
Courage	Inner	Special
Distinct	Lantern	Stars
Enlighten	Mysterious	True
Exceptional	Myths	Universe
Genuine	Newborn	Walk
Glorious	Offer	Wisdom
Heavens	Path	

The Long Glide Home

Here I dance in my white eagle feathers,
circling around, circling around.
No one knows just where we come from,
and no one knows just where we're bound.

As I'm circling, circling the boundaries of the sky,
just to stop and wonder, my spirit bound to fly.

Early I rise, high on a cool wind,
hovering silence in the cradle of space.
From a mountain aerie, my sanctuary,
the breath of my homeland, a whisper on my face.

As I'm circling higher the boundaries of the sky,
just to stop and wonder, my spirit bound to fly.

The cloud-streets of my youth now cycle behind me,
the touch of their dew was so soft on my face.
Turbulent air and the storm coming quickly
in the sky with the wind, how my heart it would race.

The thunder so mighty like a beast from within me
shaking my core and my wings start to shift.
The power of elements, the wonder of vision
as the wind, she supports me, I feel myself lift.

As I'm circling, circling, circling around,
here in the twilight, my spirit is unbound.

My kind are old, and the dream is not lasting,
where we once flourished, now you must dwell.
My brothers of wind, as we meet in passing,
as higher I climb, I wish you farewell.

As I'm circling, circling the boundaries of the sky,
just a moment's wonder, my spirit bound to fly.

—*Patrick Oliver*

Inspired Wisdom:

── ─── ──── ── ─── ───── ──
─── ─── ────── ──

```
W L L E W D E E C N A D A W L
B L A E S A N C T U A R Y H T
S R M E L T E O M E A R E I S
O O O O R D N O R T R L N S A
H O N T I I U E H E D O M P E
S G L L H N E G M A H I C E B
R E G I T E I L R E G G T R T
E H L A V L R C I H L I I E W
H W I G I E D S T F H E N H O
T N I W A R R Y N W T G O S N
A O T F E E G N I L C R I C D
E O U A S P A C E R O W S N E
F P M A S P A T R I C K I S R
I T I R I P S C L I M B V O N
```

Aerie	Eagle	Oliver
Beast	Elements	Patrick
Brothers	Feathers	Sanctuary
Circling	Glide	Space
Climb	Higher	Spirit
Core	Home	Twilight
Cradle	Lift	Vision
Dance	Long	Whisper
Dream	Mighty	White
Dwell	Mountain	Wonder

The Yoga of Breath

How do you feel about being inspired? Feels great, doesn't it? Though it may feel rare, inspiration is more common than we think, at least by one definition of the word. We each do it about 23,000 times a day. It's like breathing. Actually, it is breathing. Inspire is an action verb that means to breathe in. Breathing is an action, yet automatic.

We often inspire without even being aware of it.

Let's look at this breath-as-inspiration idea. Breath is the source of our *prana*, or vital life force. Intentional breathing practices like *pranayama*, the yoga of breath, have been scientifically demonstrated to significantly improve our overall health. Like any other yoga, a breathing practice takes intention, awareness, and repetition.

Certain styles of breathing can even help with pain management and PTSD. Breathwork is on the cutting edge of current neuroscience research around the vagus nerve, as well as effective psychological treatment techniques.

Just doing something easy like breathing through the nose instead of the mouth can increase energy and vitality, boost brainpower with extra oxygen, and reduce hypertension and stress. It also helps prevent overexertion during a workout.

Plus, we get to use our powerful, natural air-purification system, our nose. The nose is a miraculous filter lined with tiny hairs called *cilia*. The cilia have many functions. They filter, humidify, and warm or cool the air (depending on the temperature) before it enters the lungs. It is estimated that cilia protect our bodies against about twenty *billion* particles of foreign matter every day. Wow!

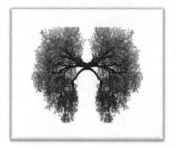

In 1243, the Arab physician Ibn al-Nafis became the first person ever to describe the breathing process in writing. Since then we've discovered that our lungs are essentially a series of connected tubes that take oxygen from the air into the blood and nourish the trillions of cells that make up our bodies. If the lungs were laid open flat, they would cover the size of a tennis court. They also clean the blood of carbon dioxide waste that is created when cells use the oxygen. The lungs look a lot like trees.

In fact, trees are often called the lungs of the Earth. What we exhale, trees inhale. Their leaves feast on carbon dioxide, and then, with help from the sun, the carbon stays in the trees, transforming into branches and trunks. Oxygen gets released for us to inhale, powering the wheel of life on Earth. Here's a fun fact: we have more than three trillion trees on our planet. That's around four hundred and some trees per person.

After we have inspired, extracted, integrated, and transmuted a breath of air, we expire what we no longer need. Seventy percent of waste is eliminated just by breathing. Vital nourishment is the result of this alchemy that happens in our lungs.

Breath is the thing that is always with you, always there for you. A breath is the first thing we take in when we are born and the last thing we release when we reach our expiration date and leave the planet. Breath is the alpha and the omega of life.

A panacea for many life circumstances, conscious breathing helps us with self-control, relaxation, and keeping calm, cool, and collected in even the most stressful situations. It can recharge us from our core. Our breath is an indicator of our mood and our mood is an indicator of our breath. This means that if we change how we breathe, we can change our mood. It also means that when our mood changes, so does our breath.

When we shift our awareness to our breathing, we rescue ourselves from the attention-splatting, distraction-filled, hustle-bustle world of information overload. That immediately brings focus to what's most important, being right here, right now. We experience the beneficial practice of focusing on one thing at a time, starting with our breath. When our thoughts are running away like the dish with the spoon, remembering to take a few deep breaths instantly brings us out of the abstract past and future and gracefully lands us into the present moment.

Are you still breathing through your nose?

Taking a breath before responding can move us from knee-jerk reaction to conscious choice in a matter of seconds. Reminding ourselves to inspire before we speak, or respond, or send that email, or start that presentation can save us all kinds of grief and regret later on. Just that quick moment of inhale and exhale can make all the difference.

Being willing and able to receive and process inspiration through our brains is a yoga. This yoga for the brain expands our intuition and helps us develop a sort of superpower. When applied to puzzles, it becomes a puzzle-vision superpower. It is beyond thinking. It is a meta-thought, *meta* meaning *beyond*. This superpower becomes our personal brain fairy godmother.

This genius X factor shows us a way through that we could not have conceived of before. A novel approach pops into our heads. Images rise up into our mind's eye. Is it clairvoyance? Guidance? Expanded intuition? Regardless of the label, the sense is that of absolute knowingness. We experience the perfect harmony of the universe; the solution comes, like magic.

This is a secret wisdom of the ages. Through conscious breathing, we can slow down our inner mind chatter enough to allow space for a unique answer to arrive smack-dab into our brains. It is nothing that we would have normally thought of. How do we do it? All we have to do is stop. Inhale. Exhale. Repeat. Inspiration is both our most essential element and our birthright.

Stay inspired. Keep breathing. It's as simple, and as complex, as that.

Go Be Awesome!

Go be awesome! Imagine if this was said to you every morning as you start your day. Being awesome means being the most loving and generous version of ourselves that we can possibly be.

Being awesome means sharing our best self with others. Sometimes it means volunteering. Sometimes it means service. Sometimes it means saying no. Sometimes it means investing in our larger communities. Sometimes it means self-care. It means coming from love when interacting with others no matter where we, or they, are.

We each have unique talents and skills that can be channeled into gifts. These gifts become amplified when shared with others. We add value to the world by accepting our true nature. When we extend the kindness of acceptance to others, we catapult our value to the world into the stratosphere.

Our work isn't so much about what we do. It is more about how we do it. Loving who we are is the key. Then it's applying that to the details. We can say "please" and "thank you" when placing an order. We can tip the driver. We can grocery shop with loving awareness of those around us. We can lend a hand or mentor someone who is new or needs help or information.

How we approach daily life matters. We matter. We are all made of matter that shares the same physical elements as the stars. Our elements are inherently awesome. Lucky for us, awesomeness is contagious.

Tag! You're it! Go be awesome!

—*Billiekai Boughton*

Inspired Wisdom:

___ __ ___ ____ __ __
_____ _____ __ __
_____

```
G Y E R E H P S O T A R T S O
I U D O I O N S P V O B T U N
F E K E H N D E L O T O O O D
T O I S E S V N E L O U Y I V
S T N E M E L E A U M G R G A
U A D R O E I R S N T H E A L
O L N V S T H A E T P T C T U
R E E I E L H W K E I O O N E
E N S C W U K A R E T N R O R
N T S E A P I E N R I E G C A
E S T N G A T A Y K V L M A C
G Z A R O T N E M I Y I L N G
T O R B A A E A R E V O L I M
A Z S M I C N D G Y K C U L B
```

Awareness	Gifts	Service
Awesome	Grocery	Shop
Billiekai	Investing	Stars
Boughton	Key	Stratosphere
Care	Kindness	Talents
Catapult	Love	Thank You
Contagious	Lucky	Tip
Driver	Matter	Value
Elements	Mentor	Volunteer
Generous	Please	

Live Strong

Unless you try to do something beyond what you already mastered, you will never grow.

—*Ronald E. Osborn*

Do you realize that you have barely scratched the surface of your potential?

We have the opportunity to do what we do best every single day. Sadly, chances are great that we don't because we are not working from our greatest assets, our strengths. Many of us don't even believe that we have them.

Most people do not have a clue what their talent powers are. They focus on their weaknesses and allow them to take hold. Change that up. Ask your friends and family what they think your strengths are. You may be surprised by what you learn.

When we accentuate our gifts, we are attracted to the work, people, and life circumstances that are in alignment with our strengths. Character strengths are manifested in thoughts, emotions, and behaviors. They are our true essence and account for us being our best selves. We improve the balance, enthusiasm, and success in our lives and can easily handle what comes up. We grow.

To reinforce your strengths, practice them in a new way. Choose your top three to five. What can you do to enhance them? Brainstorm strategies for improving core areas of your life that revolve around those assets.

When we emanate from our strengths, we become even more incredible, positive, loving, and productive people. Get strong. Get going. Get there. You can do it!

—*Barbara Eldridge*

Inspired Wisdom:

_ _ _ _ _ _ _   _ _ _ _   _ _ _ _

_ _ _ _ _ _ _ _   _ _   _ _ _

_ _ _ _ _ _ _ _ _   _ _ _ _   _ _ _   _ _ _   _ _

Cristina Smith & Rick Smith

```
B R R A D I T N E M N G I L A
A E T E F R O P S T E S S A E
T I S M A T T R A C T E D N C
A N Y T O U O O R S T R H A N
L F E N M I G D T H I A S R E
E O T O V R G U E P N T S A S
N R E A N J O C O C C T C B S
T C H A R A C T E R R C G R E
B E L I E V E I S A E B N A V
B S T R O N G V T N D A I B L
P O S I T I V E T O I L V Y O
L O V I N G G U M E B A O N V
T F A R R I A O M A L N R L E
L L Y O E T A N A M E C P B R
O U W S E G D I R D L E M D O
P O W E R S S E C C U S I O C
```

Accentuate	Character	Positive
Alignment	Core	Potential
Assets	Eldridge	Powers
Attracted	Emanate	Productive
Balance	Enhance	Reinforce
Barbara	Essence	Revolve
Behaviors	Grow	Strategies
Believe	Improving	Strong
Best	Incredible	Success
Brainstorm	Loving	Talent

The Love List

Got a busy schedule? Are you on it? How we fill up our lives is our choice. We are all human beings here on Earth with time and space to embrace.

How do you fill your calendar? What do you do with your daily twenty-four hours? We all have commitments to ourselves and others that keep us busy, both at home and at work.

Some people keep a to-do list to stay on track with the nuts and bolts of living life and prioritizing details. Sometimes that list can make us crazy with stress and feel like life is just a never-ending set of tasks. Just looking at it can make us feel overwhelmed and tired. How does your list make you feel?

Instead of a to-do list, consider creating a *love list*. Let it remind you why you love what you do. Let it support you, the people you love, and the parts of your life that you *do* love! Maybe add some items, like eleven minutes for me. Mindfulness. Family and friends. Serendipity. Fun. Community. Reading. Quiet time.

Instead of letting your to-do list be filled with problems to solve, allow your love list to evolve into the results you are creating. Make sure that taking care of you is a top priority. Find others who can help you with the tasks that are less fun for you. Focus on your strengths. Do what you do best. Live a life you love!

—*Camille Leon*

Inspired Wisdom:

__ ____ ____ _____

__ ____ ____ ___ ____ __ __

_ _____ _____ ___

```
M S S M Y S U B S T L O B Y Y
L P O T I E C I O H C N V L E
L A I S L N C O M M U N I T Y
T C Y E N U D R E T I M C G H
A E E T R S S F S V A M N Y L
L I F E I A F E U F L I W I T
L H T Q H P D R R L T O E E E
O J O R U S I N I A N E S M L
W Y S E N I E D E E V E B I U
O F N A F L E R N L N R S T D
E W M D L I C T O E A D S S E
O U L I U T L V I C R C S O H
H N M N S E E L E O N E V E C
R A Y G P R I O R I T Y S D S
C S U P P O R T E A R T H A Y
```

Allow
Bolts
Busy
Calendar
Camille
Choice
Community
Creating
Earth
Embrace

Evolve
Family
Fill
Friends
Humans
Leon
Mindfulness
Nuts
Priority
Quiet

Reading
Results
Schedule
Serendipity
Solve
Space
Support
Time

Transformations

Imagine what life would be like with more energy, peace of mind, capacity for love, and enthusiasm. Imagine what it would be like to live your best life ever.

Wellness can help us all live happier, healthier lives while shining our brightest light. It all starts when we begin to change ourselves from the inside out.

Change is a journey best navigated from the heart. The most effective transformations are realized when we embrace the fact that the body, mind, and spirit exist as one. This means that the power to overcome life's greatest challenges comes from within. Positive psychology reminds us that we're equipped with an innate will that seeks wholeness whenever we feel broken. The path of wellness offers step-by-step choices to help us transform our inner worlds and positively impact our outer worlds. Wellness acknowledges that change is inevitable. Growth is optional.

The field of mental wellness improves overall well-being and even helps people who are struggling with chronic conditions. It integrates the therapeutic benefits of mindfulness, neuroplasticity, emotional literacy, social empathy, and spiritual empowerment. When applied to our lives, these uplifting practices can result in personal and spiritual growth of the deepest kind.

As we all do our personal work and then align with others in a true heart connection, we heal and transform ourselves, each other, and our world. The most wonderful benefit of wellness happens when whole communities shine their heart lights as one. Ready, set, beam!

—*Dr. Laurie Mastrogianis*

Inspired Wisdom:

— — — — — — — — — — — — — — — — — — — —
— — — — — — — — — — — — — — — — —
— — — — — — — — — — — — — —

Cristina Smith & Rick Smith

```
B P E A C E L I T E R A C Y H
O N M W H H E O H O M L E E P
D G R E U N A T V H A R A S E
Y I O E I P W N A E S R O N V
E L F H D O L P G S T W E E I
M A S L R I P I T E R M M M T
B L N G N I S I F E O S A S I
R L A H E M F N E T G G E L S
A A R R L E P S I Y I O B A O
C I T U N N S O H N A N I U P
E C N E L T N E E Y N O G R U
D O B R L A U T I R I P S I B
N S R I L L E G H T S E S E T
I Y G R E N E H Y H T A P M E
M L I W O N D E R F U L G H T
```

Align	Happier	Mind
Beam	Heal	Peace
Benefits	Heart	Positive
Body	Imagine	Shine
Change	Inside	Social
Embrace	Laurie	Spiritual
Emotional	Literacy	Transform
Empathy	Love	Uplifting
Energy	Mastrogianis	Wonderful
Growth	Mental	

Listen to the Shaman Within

What is a shaman? Historically, a medicine man or wise woman, a keeper of traditions and dreams, a resource for the tribe. Everyone has a shaman within. We contact our inner shaman through prayer, ritual, or ceremony. It speaks with the voice of Spirit. This inner knowledge allows us to tap into the consciousness of everything and find wisdom, guidance, and healing.

One of my shamanic journeys began when I was overwhelmed and soul-deep miserable with the need for relief. My turmoil drove me to consult my inner shaman. I was kindly instructed to go for a walk and look for messages.

I stomped outdoors, tears flowing. As I walked, my downcast eyes quickly found feathers strategically placed in front of me.

I found a downy hawk feather. It spoke of a chance for a new beginning. *Embrace your innocence and trust the process.*

Next a large crow feather appeared and cawed at me. *Something needs to die to allow something else to be born. This is Universal Law.* I felt the knot in my belly tighten as my answers confirmed the path I was afraid to take.

Tears fell as I turned the corner and found the third feather, a large snowy egret feather. Truly taken aback, I stared for a long time before turning around and heading home. I'd received my answer. *Be patient, purify; what you seek will come to you.*

Now, when I'm feeling uncertain or needing comfort, I ask for more feathers to help me confirm that I'm following my soul path. And they continue to come!

—*Mara Clear Spring Cook*

Inspired Wisdom:

__ __ _____ ___
_____ ____ _ _____
___ _____

```
W M F T R I B E P R A Y E R C
Y I Q E C N A D I U G Y U O E
S S T T A C I S O S N W O R C
G O N H L T S A Y O M K R L E
N U A E I N H M M E T A A S P
I L A C W N E E R I N U E A E
L R M N D W R D R N T R T R S
A K A E H E E I P I A I U P D
E E R C C E P C R U E M R O N
H E A O I S T I R N R I A K J
H P U N S I T N T A N I W H N
T E K N O W L E D G E A F D S
A R L I T E R G E I H S T Y E
P R O C E S S N T R O F M O C
```

Ceremony	Healing	Process
Clear	Innocence	Purify
Comfort	Journeys	Ritual
Cook	Keeper	Shaman
Crow	Knowledge	Soul
Dreams	Mara	Spirit
Egret	Medicine	Spring
Feather	Path	Tribe
Guidance	Patient	Wise
Hawk	Prayer	Within

26   We Choose Our Destiny

Our ancestors may have passed on their genetic blueprint to us, but our DNA does not determine who or what we are. Neither does our upbringing. The science of genetic blueprints and how they are modified by our physical and mental environments is called *epigenetics*. Through a biology of belief, we can alter our genes and cells by intentionally changing our thoughts, words, emotions, and actions.

We select the traits we want by choosing what we see, hear, feel, eat, think, and drink. Our interactions with people matter. We actually have a set of happiness and creativity genes we can activate.

Science and shamanism show that many so-called genetic disorders and hereditary problems can be prevented and even reversed through applied epigenetics. Helpful actions include meditation and mindfulness. Energy exercises like yoga plus healthy food, air, and water have a positive impact. Loving connections and optimistic attitudes are highly beneficial for our vitality and longevity.

Our ancestors love us and want to help us heal, too. Through ancestral healing, we can clear unwanted family patterns from past generations for our entire lineage. This brings more peace into our lives now and creates new possibilities for our progeny.

Turn on your positive genes. Turn off the negative ones. Consciously select how you want to live your life. Use your choices and actions to remold and reprogram your DNA. Know that every moment of every day we get to cherry-pick our experience of well-being from the inside out.

Choose happiness, abundance, love, and health. Choose your highest destiny. Live long and prosper.

—*Ariann Thomas*

Inspired Wisdom:

— — — — — — — — — — — — — — — — — — — — —

— — — — — — — — — — — — —

— — — — — — — — — — — — — — — — — — — —

— — — — — — — —

```
H E F E I L E B B I O L O G Y
A L I N G B L U E P R I N T G
O T H O M A S U S R S F I A M
I L I C N B E S E M C V Y Y S
I S A D O U E N S D I H R E P
E Y G R E N E I I T T R L E P
E L Y V I D N E A L E O A S A
S C O P S A C E A H N C R S P
O L P L M N R E C G E E N R D
O A L A E C H D E T G O O A N
H E H I D E E V I T I S O P F
C S C I T S I M I T P O U L F
I S L L T T I N C E E G N W A
Y T O I Y R S A R I A N N S E
R V N E M A R G O R P E R H U
M Y Y T I L A T I V A N I T Y
```

Abundance	Connections	Love
Actions	Creativity	Optimistic
Ancestral	Destiny	Peace
Ariann	DNA	Positive
Belief	Energy	Prosper
Biology	Epigenetics	Reprogram
Blueprint	Happiness	Science
Cells	Healthy	Shamanism
Cherry	Lineage	Thomas
Choose	Longevity	Vitality

Abundance and Possibility

How do we create more abundance in our lives? We live in an exciting time of new creative energy and consciousness expansion. It has never been easier to attract the things and experiences that we desire. It is important to be clear on what we want.

Most of us were taught that we have to manage and control the way in which abundance comes to us. We believed that we had to go out there and get a job. We needed to do some kind of work to make money or sell something. This belief system kept our focus very small. We attracted prosperity, but only in a narrow and limited way.

If we embrace the limitless universe of possibility, we can use this new energy to expand our ideas. Our concepts about money, time, and work may become transformed.

Consider giving up the old tools and concepts. Open yourself to the idea that new forms of abundance can flow into your life. We don't have to plan it all out. Believe in miracles and angels and synchronicity and dreams. Open yourself to new opportunities. Allow yourself to create and attract abundance from a bigger, more expanded state of possibility and potential.

What if you invite your own personal belief system to expand fully and naturally? Abundance just might flow into your life in some surprising new ways!

—*Paula Wansley*

Inspired Wisdom:

— — — — — — — — — — — — — — — — —

— — — — — — — — — — — — — — — — —

— — — — — — — — — — — — — — — — —

— — — — — — — — — —

```
P A U L A N G E L S S T T E S
P Y A Y T I R E P S O R P O A
B T U B L T O C R E A T I V E
F I C T U L H E B N O X U G D
O C G A F N U L S S I L N M I
I I E G R T D F E U D I I T H
I N X W E T O A N O S M V K I
N O P P O R T U N I T I E S G
A R A O M R N A R C B T R D E
X H N E T I K P P S E L S A N
D C D E N E R G Y N L E E I N
T N E E M U N A O O I S I W N
F Y D I S I N T C C E S I O T
E S T E T I V N I L V W O L F
P O S S I B R S M A E R D L I
L I T Y M O N E Y E L S N A W
```

Abundance	Energy	Paula
Allow	Expanded	Potential
Angels	Flow	Prosperity
Attract	Fully	Surprising
Believe	Ideas	Synchronicity
Bigger	Invite	Time
Consciousness	Limitless	Transformed
Creative	Miracles	Universe
Desire	Money	Wansley
Dreams	Opportunities	Work

Create

Create a new pathway for a healthier habit today.
Hold a hand, send a prayer.
Find a partner to play with, heal with, grow with.
Paint that painting, write that book, help that other.

Create a new sensation!

Inhale. Interrupt old patterns of negativity and addictions. Exhale them out.
Breathe. Inhale deep into the belly, safe as a baby.
Create a new neural pathway in your brain for a new day of opportunity.
Listen to intuitive messages knocking on your heart's door. Invite them in.

Clear out energy that doesn't belong to you. Exhale. Take intentional action.
The power of Einstein, the energy of Mother Earth, is ready for you to tap into, and use.

Your human right is to create.
Choose what to manifest and make it so.

Breathe in. Power into your solar plexus, take hold of your body.
Focus your energy. What do I need? To heal. To create. To contribute.
Strengthen your heartstrings with unconditional love.

Your will is your magic wand.
Wave it daily to create as you please as you exhale.
Choose wisely.

You have the choice to be free. Ready?

—*Doveina Serrano*

Inspired Wisdom:

— ———— ——— ————— —— ——————
— ——— ———————— —— —— ———— ——
—————————

```
I E Y D O B T R A E H W H M E
A W X I N H A L E V R E A T N
O I H H E P D O R I W N R E E
N L S R A N T S T E I O E C R
A L E R A L Y E E F N D Y P G
R E N H A A E D E V N T A T Y
R M S E W A N S O A A I R E W
E P A H A T T H W V N W P A H
S W T G E E I N S T E I N O P
A A I V I N Y H I U N I L M T
P Y O L I C I E F E C D N B I
Y L N A C E T A E R C O H A B
O O R H E L P L P L A Y F S A
I B N G E T U B I R T N O C H
```

Body	Hand	Partner
Brain	Heal	Pathways
Contribute	Heart	Play
Create	Help	Prayer
Doveina	Hold	Sensation
Einstein	Inhale	Serrano
Energy	Love	Wave
Exhale	Magic	Wand
Focus	Manifest	Will
Habit	Paint	Write

Let Your Soul Shine

What if a magical genie appeared before you and granted you one wish? What would it be? If you're like many, your answer would be "I wish to be happy." Happiness is something we all wish for. We go through life seeking that special thing that will gift us this happiness.

We search for it high and low. Under and over. We look for it in people, in a career, in our bank accounts, in far-off lands, and in all the beautiful things we buy for ourselves. And yet, that happiness always seems to be short-lived or elusive. As soon as we get what it is that we desire, there suddenly is something else we need that we hope will grant us this happiness.

What if you didn't need to go anywhere? What if your happiness sits here in the very room you are sitting in right now? Wouldn't that be amazing?

Guess what? It's true.

Beautiful soul, you don't have to search high and low for happiness or inner joy. It has always existed right inside of you. How do you find it? Take the time to connect within. Discover a light unlike anything you've ever seen.

Breathe in deeply your magnificence. Feel the peace and contentment that flows through you.

Stop the wild goose chase. The light we've all been so furiously seeking has been within us all along.

It's *you*. Cultivate that light. Shine that light. Sit back in awe as you witness joy bloom from within that beautiful soul of yours.

—*Shari Alyse*

Inspired Wisdom:

＿＿＿＿＿＿＿＿ ＿＿＿＿ ＿＿＿＿＿
＿＿＿＿＿＿ ＿＿＿ ＿＿＿＿＿＿＿＿＿ ＿＿＿
＿＿＿＿＿ ＿＿＿＿ ＿＿＿

```
D S I C G E N I E S H A R I S
C H O V O D E R L A C I G A M
Y I O U L N S W O L F R O L E
I N S I D E N I G G H T O T T
W E W I T H I E N N N A S N A
H M A G N I F I C E N C E M V
A H S I W S K A M T D I O L I
P L S U D E P T L S M O E B T
P E I S E E N E E Y L N R A L
I T C S E E T A C B S E I E U
N L T A T N R N H I A E S E C
E W U N E C T J A T A O E T A
S R O O H P O I H R L L D F W
S C D W S Y I E W T G H J I E
F E E L U F I T U A E B O G Y
```

Alyse	Flows	Peace
Awe	Genie	Search
Beautiful	Gift	Seeking
Bloom	Goose	Shari
Breathe	Granted	Shine
Connect	Happiness	Soul
Contentment	Inside	Special
Cultivate	Joy	Wild
Desire	Magical	Wish
Feel	Magnificence	Witness

Celebrate!

When's the last time you celebrated yourself? Was it an official time like a birthday or just because? Can you not even remember the last time you celebrated yourself just because? Then it's been way too long.

Celebration is an important key to happiness and resilience. What's in your life right now worth celebrating? Celebrate it!

Stop and celebrate each goal achieved and each instance that makes you laugh or smile. It can be silly or life-changing. You got the job! You aced the puzzle! You got that overfilled closet finally cleaned out! All excellent reasons. Think of yours.

Some days a quiet celebration is in order for the incredible strength and courage you showed by getting up and out of bed when you really didn't want to. Only you truly know how much that took.

Celebrate accomplishments at each step. The process of celebration actually slows us down long enough to notice the momentum of our path. That act of stopping could be for a minute or an hour or a day or longer. By doing this, we make better choices. We make them from a place of joy and self-love and from the heart.

Celebration rituals are individual and need to fit you. For some it's a dance. For some a party. Some celebrate with a favorite food. Some curl up with a good book. It's whatever floats your boat. Make it excellent in your terms.

Our quality of life improves greatly when we stop to appreciate what we have created at each step along the way.

What if our whole lives became a journey of celebration? Wouldn't that be awesome?

—Cheryl Marks Young

Inspired Wisdom:

_ _ _ _ _ _ _ _ _ _ _   _ _ _   _ _ _   _ _ _
_ _ _ _ _ _   _ _ _ _ _ _   _ _ _ _ _   _ _
_ _ _ _ _ _ _ _ _ _   _ _ _ _   _ _ _

```
G O A L R C Y T R A P P G E L
E K E Y I B R R A T O N I N G
T B I R T H D A Y T U H E B I
E G Q E U A W E S O M E A N D
T T U H A P C H Y I A M J L I
I T A C L P E T L N R O O E T
R H L I S I L I N D K M U G S
O K I E C N E I L I S E R H E
V O T C L E B P S V U N N S E
A O Y N X S R L P I E T E R I
F B O A T S A P R D E U Y N C
F O O D E H T A P U M M O R E
I M P R O V E S U A C E B J O
N O T I C E X C E L L E N T Y
```

Appreciate	Excellent	Marks
Awesome	Favorite	Momentum
Because	Food	Notice
Birthday	Goal	Party
Boat	Happiness	Path
Book	Heart	Quality
Celebrate	Improves	Resilience
Cheryl	Individual	Rituals
Curl	Journey	Stop
Dance	Key	Young

Curiosity as Inspiration

What inspires us to greet each day with grace? Is there a secret key? A great diet? A supportive partner? Exercise? Plenty of money? Satisfying work? These are all helpful, but it may be a surprise to discover that the master key to the castle of a vibrant, healthy, and fulfilling life is something we are all born with: curiosity.

Curiosity is a strong desire to want to learn something. As babies we had natural curiosity to figure out how the world works. It's the way we learned how to be a human. Whether it was cultivated or discouraged as we grew up, somewhere deep down inside of us, that spark is still there.

No matter how busy we are, it's time to give ourselves permission to dig within our hearts, minds, and souls to fan that curious spark into a flame of desire. That flame will warm every moment of our lives. Follow your inspirations and interests. They fuel the drive to want to boldly go where you haven't gone before. Consider it a clue in solving the ever-deepening puzzle of you. After all, puzzles come in all different forms, and research says they are good for us. Tap into your underlying quest for knowledge to work this challenge and get inspired.

Who? What? When? Where? How? Why? Inquiring minds want to know. Exercising and stretching our inquisitiveness becomes a yoga for our brains. It leads us to our inspiration. This mental yoga not only enriches our lives, it actually hones and improves our minds and bodies by kindling and feeding the fire of that creative spark. Inspiration stimulates curiosity and curiosity provides us with the prepared mind inspiration seeks.

There are different flavors of curiosity. If you're intellectual, you'll go home and do the research. If you're perceptual, you might go traveling to foreign countries and taste different foods. If you are social, you want to know what other people are thinking and doing. If you are experientially curious, you are willing to take physical, social, and financial risks to gain varied, complex, and intense experiences.

Creativity comes from curiosity. The more interested we are, the more we experience and learn. The more we experience and learn, the more connections our brains are able to make. And with more connections, we can find new solutions to problems or see things no one else can see. Curiosity is deliciously thought-provoking, a powerful feast for the brain.

We digest our mind food at our own internal pace. Some of the tidbits energize us right away. Others are more on a slow burn or simmer, and reveal their results at unexpected times. How many of us experience our best ideas while driving to work, taking a walk, or standing in the shower? Or watching a movie, doing the dishes, or reading a book that has nothing to do with the problem just solved? Our brains are processing vastly more information than we're even aware of. And sometimes it's making connections between things we weren't even looking for at the time.

Curiosity just gets curiouser and curiouser the further down the rabbit hole we go.

According to the National Institutes of Health, we actually become wiser with age. Flexing our brains has been shown to reduce the risk of Alzheimer's, dementia, and other diseases that strike terror into our hearts and minds.

Researchers from Columbia University and the New York State Psychiatric Institute found that even the oldest brains they studied produced new brain cells. That's our amazing neuroplasticity in action. This natural process, affirmed by research in the last fifty years, acknowledges that our brains are superbly supple and form new neural connections throughout life. These provide us with an ever-evolving brain when we give it the juice it needs to power the process of making new cells and connections. We, and our brains, are more fascinating and capable than we can possibly imagine.

How does it feel when we are curious? Energized, certainly. There's an urgency, an excitement, and a stimulation that propels us to explore and discover. What's happening in our brains when we are feeling this way? Like a good puzzle, neuroscience reports that curiosity activates the dopamine bliss center of the brain, which functions to maintain motivation and drive towards a reward. That means that as we are following our road to find out, our brains are encouraging us by releasing feel-good chemicals.

To keep your brain supple and happily serving you, dive into your need to know. What have you always wanted to find out about? What have you always wanted to do, but haven't because you thought you would be judged for not being good at it? Free yourself to explore the windy, curvy paths where curiosity leads and inspiration lurks.

What is it for you? How do you choose? What inspires you? What are you curious about? What floats your boat and fills you with a sense of delight and excitement? Want to learn to identify birds or butterflies or plants or minerals? Have you always wanted to play an instrument, paint, salsa dance, or learn another language? Does the idea of kayaking down a river thrill you? Ever wanted to go up in a balloon? Did you always suspect you would be really good at something, but were afraid to try it out? Or didn't have the time? Now's the perfect time. Even if it's just some online research or a book from the library to get you started, it's a beginning.

Turn the curiosity master key to open your personal treasure chest of wonder and reap the rewards in all aspects of your life. Let your inspiration lead you to somewhere amazing. You'll be glad you did.

Inspiration from the Vineyard

Know where your wine comes from? Welcome to the vineyard, an allegory for life.

The grape vineyard shows us that change is opportunity. When the spring weather warms, the buds along the pruned canes burst, unfurling into tiny green leaves with rose-tipped edges. The air is vibrant with the chirping and twittering of the many birds who call the vineyard home. A bluebird lands on a trellis wire in a flash of color. A swallow swoops and swirls, catching insects. High above, a red-tailed hawk circles. Joy and hope fill the air.

By summer the canes fill the trellis, the grape crop has set, and maturity lies ahead. Yet, ever present is the threat of disease, insect damage, or harsh weather. The grapes can be harmed by sunburn on hot days, desiccation from hot winds, or frost just before harvest. The vines must withstand whatever Mother Nature throws at them.

Approximately one hundred days after bloom, the vineyard rings with the chatter of harvest. Pickers run to dump buckets brimming over with dark purple clusters into the large totes. The rumble of tractors ferrying the totes to the winery fills the air. When it's over, the vines seem to breathe a collective sigh of relief. Their work is done. The leaves turn yellow, bathing the vineyard in a golden hue.

The leaves slowly waft to the ground, until the vines are totally bare. The vineyard has become a skeleton. But the silence of winter is deceiving. Underground, the vines regenerate. Come spring, they will revive. Every year represents a fresh start and renewed hope.

Cheers!

—*Susan Sokol Blosser*

Inspired Wisdom:

———— —— —— ———————— —————
—— ——————— —— ———————— ——
————————— —— ————————

```
L C I S W I N E R Y S F H E I
S A A E K S N V C P O E A N D
L N E R D E I D U R K S R S E
Y E C U Y B L R R C O L V R G
T S B T R B P E E A L P E O N
I F G A R L L S T O Y H S W A
N T N N E B I O H O T E T T H
U T W O L L A W S O N C N O C
T M A T L U U R M S H Y I I T
R E G E N E R A T E E Y O S V
O M R T O B D O E R M R E J E
P T O G N I P R I H C V A N P
P C Y O T R S O R H A W K E A
O N G O L D E N E E V I V E R
W E P O H B A L L S U S A N G
```

Bloom	Grape	Regenerate
Blosser	Harvest	Revive
Bluebird	Hawk	Skeleton
Buds	Hope	Sokol
Canes	Joy	Susan
Change	Leaves	Swallow
Cheers	Mother	Trellis
Chirping	Nature	Vibrant
Crop	Opportunity	Vineyard
Golden	Purple	Winery

Soul Evolution

We are the sum total of all that we have experienced.

We can compost what we've gained by analyzing and processing all that we have been through, from absolute bliss to the darkest nastiness in our lives. Our futures emerge from that enriched soil. We germinate our new lives from all that has gone before.

Trust in Divine Wisdom to guide and guard along the path. Take advantage of and honor your sacred inner knowing, and the teachings of those who have come before.

We have and can spring back into shape. Our resilience is proven. It's all in the recovery.

The petals of the lotus flower open up to the light one by one. Lotus roots live in mud and muck and rough conditions. We flower and bloom from the nourishment provided by the fertilizer of our past.

Just as fruit trees go from seed to sprout to tree to bloom to fruit to harvest to fall to dormant, we cycle through stages. Like the seasons, recognize that circumstances come to pass, they do not come to stay.

Dig deep down inside and cultivate your innermost understanding and truth to bring forth the whole spectrum of your life, from light to dark.

Emerge anew, grateful for the process.

—*Denise Lewis Premschak*

Inspired Wisdom:

__ ____ _____ ____ __
_____ _____
_____ __ ___ _____
__ __ ____

```
M H T U R T L R O N O H Y S O
U L D I V I N E B L A G O S D
S O S E M S I C W R N E T O S
O M E Y E B R N V I R R R I T
L K A H C S M E R P S M L R O
S I S A N T S I N G A I F E O
P U O P T T U L N N R N T W R
R E N N E S O I T U I A R O B
O T S I S C W S L E V T S L L
U H S I E O T E O I S E D F O
T B L O N F E R T I L I Z E O
D B Y K P A L L U L L A N S M
W I S D O M U P S M E C T E S
O F G M Y C O F R U I T P A D
S D E R C A S C S L A T E P T
```

Bliss	Germinate	Sacred
Bloom	Harvest	Seasons
Compost	Honor	Seed
Cultivate	Inner	Soil
Denise	Knowing	Spectrum
Dig	Lewis	Sprout
Divine	Lotus	Total
Dormant	Petals	Truth
Fertilize	Premschak	Wisdom
Flower	Resilience	
Fruit	Roots	

Listen Within

I grew up in a home where parents hardly ever talked to one another. A direct answer was never given to a question asked. Conflicting messages were given regarding God and religion. I learned to look within myself at a very young age.

I didn't realize it at the time, but what I was doing was meditating. I started this by age four or five. It came very naturally to me to sit quietly, blocking out the world around me. I listened with my mind, not with my ears. I envisioned the most extraordinary things. I was only six when I received a message not to believe everything I heard. I was told to "take it with a grain of salt."

I didn't know that expression at the time, so I knew this message came from outside of me, even though I found it within. I was eight when I was told that I would write and publish a book someday. I just published my fifth.

Looking within and really listening to that still small voice allows and encourages all of us to follow our dreams no matter how impossible they may seem.

Listen.

Sit quietly and still and deeply listen.

The still small voice from within speaks volumes to our lives and souls. Hear it and pay attention to it to live a remarkable life. Follow your dreams with confidence.

—*Dennel B. Tyon*

Inspired Wisdom:

— — — — — — — —   — — —   — — — — — — —

— — — — — — —   — — —   — — — — — — — —

— — — — —   — — — — —   — — — — —

```
B S T I C L H S I L B U P I Q
F O L L O W E M L L N N M E U
S S O A N N A D E S L P O L I
G I L K F N R E N S O A I Y E
N R L L I T S O C S S M S T
E G A H D S I V S S T A L S L
A N T I E T E I O E M U G S Y
M I N D N M B G N L O A P E P
W T L E C L S I A S U E E F Y
T A T L E L B A K R A M E R H
E T B E E E A U L K U T E I D
A I F N U T L Q S T U O I S S
E D E N V I S I O N E D C I T
I E N E N R E C I O V E T N R
V M O D I W C D E E P L Y E E
```

Attention	Hear	Sit
Book	Impossible	Small
Confidence	Listen	Souls
Deeply	Meditating	Speaks
Dennel	Message	Still
Dreams	Mind	Tyon
Envisioned	Publish	Voice
Encourages	Quietly	Volumes
Follow	Remarkable	Within
Grain	Salt	Write

Regain Your Power

What is life about? It's about love, self-discovery, evolving, and sharing. Life is about living from the heart, knowing your truth, and having compassion.

Life has ups and downs. We are given opportunities to learn and guidance to move forward on our evolutionary paths. The more open we are to possibilities, the more we can see. When we expand our reality boxes, we can manifest our hearts' desires.

We are all energetically connected with life, Earth, and the Universe. We exist in a collective energy field of strength and wisdom. This field surrounds us and is within us. You are part of it. Search within for your answers. Many of the answers we seek do not come from the brain. Ask your heart and Spirit for assistance.

We are powerful beings, more powerful than what we have been told. See beyond the day-to-day physical world into the bigger collective picture. It is time for us to remove the limiting beliefs that hold us back. We have dragged those stories and illusions with us for far too long. They no longer serve us.

Make yourself a priority. Believe in yourself more. Have love, compassion, and patience for yourself. It starts with each and every one of us. It is only after we take care of ourselves that these energies genuinely overflow to others, nature, Earth, and the Universe.

Open to yourself and regain your power. Connect to your heart and soul. Enjoy life's magical journey. Release. Reconnect. Rejoice!

—*Diana Borges*

Inspired Wisdom:

__ _____ ___
_____ _____ _ __ ___
____ _____ ___ ___

```
D I A N A M Y T I L A E R R I
D G E T E M A M B S R A C E S
L U E S T S O G P N E H S J E
E I E E M D A I I V I T A O X
I D G F S N R E E C R A W I O
F A I I F I P I L E A I G C B
I N W N T E L R N E T L H E C
E C N A T E V G I H R C B T R
E E I M B N T I I O R G R I S
B L U O S H A N T A R U M Y R
O P R E C O N N E C T I G A E
R N O D H A V S E H E R T L W
G C O W M E N J O Y E L O Y S
E E C N E I T A P N P V L A N
S S S I O R N F E O E R A O A
L L P I C T U R E T R A E H C
```

Answers	Heart	Regain
Believe	Love	Rejoice
Borges	Magical	Release
Boxes	Manifest	Search
Collective	Patience	Soul
Diana	Picture	Spirit
Energy	Power	Strength
Enjoy	Priority	Truth
Field	Reality	Wisdom
Guidance	Reconnect	Within

Fluidity

When life gets tough, what keeps you moving? What motivates you to stay positive, or even get up in the morning? It's easy to stay cozy in our comfort zones. Sometimes our comfort zones stop working. True growth comes from perseverance and the courage to try something new when the old is no longer effective.

Assess what isn't working for you. Thank it for its lesson, light a match, set it on fire, and walk happily onward. Use your past experiences as fuel to guide your next idea, relationship, or project. Focus on what you can do, not what you can't. Listen to your heart. Let your heart make the decisions and your brain create the strategies. Enter that flow and don't resist what is. Sometimes easier said than done.

Lean on your spiritual practice to show you the way. Patience and compassion for ourselves help the journey along. Recognize dissatisfaction. Accept change without frustration. Know that true success comes from doing what you love and living in alignment with your true self.

Dream big. Surround yourself with people who want to see you grow. Find people who push you, in a good way, to move out of that cozy comfort zone. Hang with the ones who inspire you and show you what's possible. Make them proud. Make yourself proud. Keep going! Use grit and determination. There is no limit to what we can achieve when we embrace the fluidity of change.

—*Sarah Burchard*

Inspired Wisdom:

— — — — — — — —   — —   — — — — —   — — —
— — — — — — —   — —   — — —   — — — —   — — —
— — — —   — —   — — — —   — — — — — —

```
R E S T H G I L S M S E P M B
B R A I N E R U T P D O R Y E
U N R N J O C J I O E Y A Z T
R H A O E C S R O E T P C O R
C E H I E R I S S U E E T C E
H P O S I T I V E Z R N I T C
A A S S U L S F O L M N C S N
R E L A T I O N S H I P E Y E
D O L P U W E V A D N T L Y I
R K H M S E I G E T A R T S T
A T E O A H E A P V T T A T A
W H A C T T Y T I D I U L F P
N P R O J E C T P R O U D O Y
O O T U R F O H G U N T U R E
A L I G N M E N T R O F M O C
```

Alignment	Heart	Positive
Brain	Idea	Practice
Burchard	Journey	Project
Comfort	Lesson	Proud
Compassion	Light	Relationship
Cozy	Love	Sarah
Determination	Match	Spiritual
Fire	Motivates	Strategies
Fluidity	Onward	Success
Grit	Patience	Zone

Awareness and Self-Love

Self-love means being patient with ourselves when handling life's challenges. When a situation or conflict arises, take time to step back and examine the feelings. *Why do I feel this way?* This gives us an opportunity to explore new levels of our inner world. See other individuals not as who they are, but as mirrors reflecting back areas within ourselves needing extra love and attention.

We are all onions. Every obstacle is a chance to peel back a new layer of understanding, including our feelings and emotional triggers.

We become empowered to create happiness in our lives when we illuminate those feelings that steal our joy. We face the feelings and allow them to pass through us, instead of staying suppressed within. This brings us freedom.

Stay aware and mindful of feelings. They help us to see our triggers first, before reacting to situations. We can then shift from being victims of circumstance to co-creators of our lives. We are willing to look at our reflections and ask why. When we are brave enough to travel down the path of awareness, we remove the shackles of the past that hold us back. Blame or other avoidance tactics don't serve us.

When we take responsibility for our lives, we are choosing to step into the light and shine. How can you love yourself more today? Do it.

—*Nadia Kim*

Inspired Wisdom:

_ _ _ _ _   _ _ _   _ _ _ _   _ _ _ _ _ _ _   _ _
_ _ _ _ _   _ _ _ _   _ _ _
_ _ _ _ _ _   _ _ _ _   _ _ _   _ _ _

```
T S R U L S P A T I E N T Y T
A L L O W A S N O I N O T P N
D L V E V A R B O G V I H E E
A E Y W V F O U R N L T T E S
E W H D F E M O T I O N A L L
T Y A E R E L K B D F E P U T
H E P R E L O I S N T T S F H
G N P E E I S M I A R T M D N
I I I W D N E L N T I A I N I
L M N O O G E I K S G I T I E
E A E P M S M S T R G D C M H
V X S M E U B R S E E A I I G
A E S E L H T S T D R N V A R
R E F L E C T I O N S H I F T
T M I R R O R S Y U O U A R E
```

Allow	Illuminate	Patient
Attention	Kim	Peel
Awareness	Levels	Reflections
Brave	Light	Responsibility
Emotional	Love	Shift
Empowered	Mindful	Travel
Examine	Mirrors	Triggers
Feelings	Nadia	Understanding
Freedom	Onions	Victims
Happiness	Path	Why

Childhood's End

There are so many problems in our world. We have epidemic levels of anxiety, depression, suicide, addiction, and mental health disorders. How did this happen? What can we do about it?

It all starts in childhood.

Childhood isn't always idyllic. It can be filled with confusion and turmoil. The child's experience is vastly different than the adult's experience. The child's behavior adapts to avoid displeasing the parents.

The authentic self of the child can go dormant. Children strive to be good enough, or perfect enough, or obedient enough to please. Sometimes nothing works. Internal suffering settles in as a normal way of life. A vicious cycle can be born.

Sound familiar? The child yearns to be accepted, as is.

The good news is that it is never too late to love, acknowledge, and accept our internal children exactly as they are. In all their authentic beauty and rage. The act of witnessing and acknowledging the truth of our inner children can create profound changes.

The child is seen. And heard. And acknowledged. And allowed and encouraged to be. However he or she chooses. We don't attempt to change or cajole, negotiate, or discipline. We witness.

The authentic self is powerful and potent. If forced into the wrong-sized box, destruction ensues. Remove the box and find the real self within. Nurture it. Give it time, space, and unconditional love to evolve. Watch it emerge from its unique cocoon, transformed from caterpillar to beautiful butterfly.

—*Jennifer Whitacre*

Inspired Wisdom:

_ _ _ _ _ _ _ _   _ _ _ _   _ _ _ _   _ _ _
_ _ _ _ _ _ _ _   _ _ _ _   _ _ _ _
_ _ _ _ _ _ _ _   _ _ _ _

```
H S E R C A T I H W W F L E S
E D U U F F U E S I E R I A N
A E G N E B U T T E R F L Y A
R G N C O Q E N H D E L S C W
D A H O I O E A E E O N K N P
Y R O N R S C U U W N N R T R
N O N I E C F D C W Y T I E F
W C A T E R P I L L A R R C O
T N I I T R H E N Y E U O C U
R E U O E R D A U N T V X A N
U T C N H G L U F R E W O P D
T E N A E M I T U N T J B L I
H I C L P S E N P O T E N T L
F M R O F S N A R T D L I H C
```

Accept	Encouraged	Self
Acknowledge	Heard	Space
Allowed	Inner	Time
Authentic	Jennifer	Transform
Beauty	Love	Truth
Box	Nurture	Unconditional
Butterfly	Potent	Unique
Caterpillar	Powerful	Whitacre
Child	Profound	Witness
Cocoon	Seen	

Keep Choosing Forgiveness

How we go through the ups and downs of life is more important than the ups and downs themselves. Difficulties arise. We make mistakes. We don't know what to do next. Do we live with compassion, love, and forgiveness, or with judgment and self-criticism?

Perhaps we judge ourselves harshly for not knowing the way forward. Sometimes we might even feel as if we are living in an ongoing crisis of uncertainty. When we come to life like this, we invite anxiety and panic, the opposite direction of the peace we are ultimately seeking.

Ignoring angst and tension and *pushing through* experiences leads to more challenges. Consider a pause. Take a breath. Acknowledge yourself. *I'm having a really hard time with this right now.* Meet yourself gently. Ask yourself, "What would it look like and feel like to comfort myself in this moment?"

Bring kindness and understanding into the picture. Embrace all of who you are, including your shortcomings and foibles.

When we forgive ourselves first, then we can move on to forgiving others. Forgiveness is the root of compassion. Forgiving ourselves is often the hardest.

Keep choosing compassion.

Keep choosing forgiveness.

Keep choosing love.

—*Elizabeth Kipp*

Inspired Wisdom:

___ _____ __ _____ __
_____ ___ ___ __ _____
____ __ ____ ___ _____
___

```
C T S E D R A H L L P A U S E
E O B T L T H E E I R N E B F
E P M R E I A C C F D E O I N
N F F F E E Z T A E A R R G T
H O O O O A U A R G A S E N G
D R I S R R T S B D T N D N L
E W B S E G T H M E T T I I T
B A L E S A I E E L T S S E G
I R E N N A P V Y W O H N L N
W D S D W I P O E O F T O O R
T H I N O T I M H N E V C M E
F N R I D E K C O K E O U M T
G N I K E E S H E C L S P I N
S I D E O M I S T A K E S U T
```

Acknowledge	First	Meet
Breath	Foibles	Mistakes
Choosing	Forgiveness	Move
Comfort	Forward	Pause
Compassion	Gently	Picture
Consider	Hardest	Root
Downs	Kindness	Seeking
Elizabeth	Kipp	Understanding
Embrace	Life	Ups
Feel	Love	

Joy Is Your Birthright

You, beloved one, are a precious child of the Divine. You are a unique creation. In all the world there is no one else just like you. You are one of a kind. See that you are a gem, a treasure, a precious blessing. Your life matters. Your life matters more than you realize. You are a bright light in this world. Shine that light as only you can.

A team of angels surrounds you always, even if you aren't sure about them. Your angels have loved you since before you were born. Call upon them. They are always available to you. Let go of the idea that you are taking them away from more important work by asking for their help. The angels are omnipotent and are not bound by space and time.

Your angels are pure, unconditional love. Their messages are only loving.

Life is meant to be full of joy. Joy is your birthright. It is your essence. Joy is who you are. You are worthy. You are deserving. As a beloved child of the Divine, a life of joy is your legacy and your inheritance.

May you flourish in joy, in love, in all that lights up your beautiful heart. Thank you for being you and sharing your bright light with the world. You help make it a better place.

—*Janette Stuart*

Inspired Wisdom:

___ ___ _____ __ ____
____ ____ __ ___ __ _
_____ _____ __ ___
_____

```
B Y O S E G A S S E M U F A S
E R M E M E A T E N T L T P B
A N G E L S U N O T O L A I R
U V L E G A Y O O U T C U R I
T L A T R A E H R I E E I F G
I E N T O M N I P O T E N T H
F I O B N T S M J O C A Y A T
U A I S L H R A A N B G E P J
L N T T E E L E A Y N O E R V
S L I G H T S T A I H S E E C
R D D Q C A I S R S S T Y C H
E I N L U R N A I E U C R I D
T O O F E E H K N N A R E O T
T H C H E S D C I G G M E U W
A G N I V R E S E D I V I S N
M I U E W O R L D T E N I H S
```

Angels	Inheritance	Space
Beautiful	Janette	Stuart
Blessing	Legacy	Team
Bright	Light	Thank
Creation	Matters	Time
Deserving	Messages	Treasure
Essence	Omnipotent	Unconditional
Flourish	Precious	Unique
Gem	Sharing	World
Heart	Shine	Worthy

The Light Within

Let the light within come out to play.
It is with us every place we go.
It is carried as an inner glow.
It is something that we all know.
Let it show, let it show, let it show.

What is there that I cannot seem to see?
Is it way too deep inside of me?
If it is something we all are searching for,
why then is it so cloistered at the core?

Oh, let our lights meet.
This is that which we all seek.
Let our souls touch.
Together we can give so much more than we ever have before.
We can let the distance slip away, with everything we do and say,
we emerge as a single ray.
The light within.

Let it shine. Let it shine. Let it shine.
This luminescent inner beam
reveals the road that leads to dreams,
in spite of how things sometimes seem.
It's in you and it's in me. Smile.
Set it free. Let it be.

Shine on, in song,
we belong, and love is the way.
Fear not, you've got everything it takes,
we've got everything it makes
when the light within comes out to play.
Let the light within come out to play.

—*Kiva*

Inspired Wisdom:

_ _ _ _ _   _ _ _ _   _ _ _ _ _   _ _ _   _ _ _ _ _
_ _ _   _ _ _ _ _   _ _ _ _ _ _   _ _ _

```
D A O R S H L E T E E M I N
D E E A Y O S O D U Y R L I
E C R V G H M T V I T A S A
I L O I W T A N E E S L L E
R O C K O O E E N L A N M P
R I D E H G R C G E G E I I
A S T E S E D S V N R N N O
C T U R C T H E T G O N I H
G E G F E H R N E S E L O S
N R P L B E U I L R S E E K
O E A E O R S M E C A L P B
S D A Y E W A U N I H T I W
R M O U N D D L S M I L E Y
O U S E A R C H I N G I V E
```

Beam	Glow	Reveals
Belong	Inner	Road
Carried	Inside	Searching
Cloistered	Kiva	Seek
Core	Love	Show
Deep	Luminescent	Single
Dreams	Meet	Smile
Emerge	Place	Song
Free	Play	Together
Give	Ray	Within

Lotus Wisdom

The beautiful flower on the cover is a lotus. Long a symbol of wisdom, peace, and spirituality, few flowers have inspired hearts, minds, and souls throughout the ages like this gorgeous bloom. It is one of the most powerful flower symbols on Earth and among the oldest plants on the planet.

With more than a thousand types of flowers, there is a variety of lotus on every continent except Antarctica. A lotus seed can wait to germinate for over two centuries and has a unique life cycle. It has an undeniable will to live. Its roots are based in mud and some varieties submerge every night into murky water. Undeterred by this dirty environment, the lotus miraculously reblooms, pristine, the next morning. It continues to resurrect itself, coming back just as beautiful as it was last seen.

The lotus flower's daily resurrection is considered symbolic of renewal. It astonishes us with its ability to dip into the grime and revitalize itself unscathed, embodying an incredible daily cycle of life, death, and sudden, immaculate rebirth.

Lotus wisdom shows us we can overcome even the most difficult circumstances and feel the innate beauty life can offer. A return to serenity is possible. Many associate this flower with an unwavering faith that blossoms from within, petal by petal.

The flower was held sacred from remotest antiquity by the Hindus, Buddhists, Egyptians, and other ancient cultures. The lotus is mentioned in the Bible, revered in China and Japan, and was adopted as a Christian emblem by the Greek and Latin churches, which later replaced it with the water lily. Symbolically, the lotus and water lily are somewhat merged.

This merging can create all kinds of confusion in the lotus/water lily department. Some of this stems (pardon the pun) from the fact that the Egyptian lotus is actually a water lily. Water lilies float on the surface of the water while lotuses can bloom above the surface and have a different kind of seedpod.

Whichever they are, the flowers are beautiful; stunning, really. And they grow from the muck and mud. The sublime beauty emerging from the muck down below is a metaphor we can all get behind. The worst compost of our lives can become and help create the most beautiful flowers as we bloom as people. No mud, no lotus. Makes you think, doesn't it?

It begins to make more sense why this flower is such a beloved symbol to so many cultures. Some of the most famous water lilies of all time were painted by Claude Monet and given "like a bouquet of flowers" to France to celebrate the end of World War I on November 11, 1918. Yet again the lotus/water lily comes forth as a profound symbol for peace.

Lotuses historically have an extremely esoteric side, being beloved by metaphysicians throughout time. A symbol of revival, purity, and serenity, this flower is one of the eight auspicious symbols in both Chinese and Tibetan Buddhist iconography. The ancient Egyptians used the stylized water lily/lotus extensively as a symbol of the sun, creation, and rebirth in paintings and carvings on the walls of temples and tombs.

In Hindu culture, it is said that gods and goddesses sat on lotus thrones as a symbol of enlightenment. According to Buddhist myth, the Buddha appeared atop a floating lotus, and his first footsteps on Earth left lotus blossoms. The thousand-petaled lotus represents spiritual illumination.

These deep spiritual meanings gave rise to a way of sitting known as the lotus position. Many of us sit this way as part of our yoga practice. The legs are crossed and tucked in a way that makes the bent knees look like flower petals.

Lotuses are used to symbolize our personal energy centers, the *chakras*. Chakra is a Sanskrit word, *cakra*, that means *wheel*. It is a spinning vortex of energy that's an inch or two away from the body, that looks kind of like a wheel, thus the name. The chakra system originated in India between 1500 and 500 BCE.

The chakras play an important yet subtle role in our vitality and health. They have two essential functions. Chakras convert the motion of life force, *prana*, into an energy fuel supply for our overall physical health. That fuel is then transported and distributed throughout the body through millions of channels called *nadis*. Secondly, they assist in the development of our mental, emotional, and spiritual awareness.

There are a specific number of lotus petals, from four to nine hundred seventy-two, associated with each individual chakra. When activated, each lotus petal of the chakra can be thought of as opening and blooming along with a person's energy.

CHAKRAS INFORMATION

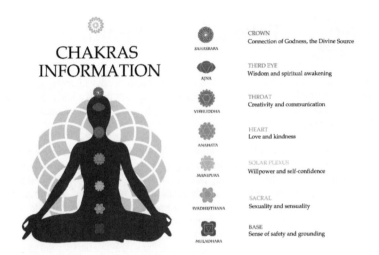

CROWN
Connection of Godness, the Divine Source

SAHASRARA

THIRD EYE
Wisdom and spiritual awakening

AJNA

THROAT
Creativity and communication

VISHUDDHA

HEART
Love and kindness

ANAHATA

SOLAR PLEXUS
Willpower and self-confidence

MANIPURA

SACRAL
Sexuality and sensuality

SVADHISTHANA

BASE
Sense of safety and grounding

MULADHARA

Lotuses inspire us to blossom where we are, no matter how seemingly impossible the odds. We are able to direct the energy of our lives, charge ourselves up, thrive, and bloom. We may end each day and intentionally submerge into the depths of transformative rest to be reborn anew beautifully in the morning.

Enjoy the serenity of this flower and this symbol. The lotus has so much to teach us. Remember, no mud, no lotus. Let the compost of your past create the gorgeous blooms of your future. Imagine your chakras spinning in elegant harmony. Allow your own internal beauty, determination, and strength to rise toward the sun, flourish, and flower magnificently.

Take a Leap of Faith

Sometimes in life, we feel stuck. We follow our routine, day after day, year after year. We just exist in a job, or a relationship, or a town that we know is not right for us. We do this because it's comfortable. It's familiar. It's safe. Change is hard. Change is uncomfortable.

In order to live to our fullest potential, it helps to recognize key moments in life that give us the opportunity to take a leap of faith. Maybe that leap is leaving a bad marriage. Or quitting a job to start a business. Or moving to a place that you feel called to. Or maybe it's as simple as starting a new hobby, or volunteering for a political campaign or nonprofit. No matter what that voice inside you is telling you to do, stop ignoring it. It may sound crazy or impossible, but it's from the voice of your spirit. Maybe it has a point? At least worth considering?

Growth doesn't happen in times of mediocrity. It does not emerge from comfort or good enough. True growth comes from our most challenging times. In order to reach our full potential, it is essential that we step outside of our comfort zones to follow the dream that is inside of each of us.

We all tell ourselves that we're not good enough, or smart enough, or talented enough to make it happen. But we are. Only you have the power to take that leap of faith and soar to your highest potential.

—Valerie Costa

Inspired Wisdom:

———— —————————— ————
——— ———————— ————— —————— ——
————————— ——— —
—————— ——————

```
L E N T A P E Z I N G O C E R
F P O W E R E A R L E H S S L
Y W N M O V I N G I A P M A C
N I P N T F A M I L I A R O T
H D R E A M E L L U N K N D O
W V O L U N T E E R I N G E N
W I F A E T N L S R T H L T F
A I I N G R B R P I B T N H
H I T T I N Y A U O I E U E O
E R S N T E O T M S L R F L B
A C G E U S N R S S I D I A B
A S I T O P P O R T U N I T Y
H T W O R G P F F U L L E S T
J U O P V M Y M H I G H E S T
F C Y T I R C O I D E M U L S
H K E A T S O C R A Z Y A R T
```

Business	Highest	Routine
Campaign	Hobby	Smart
Challenging	Impossible	Soar
Comfortable	Mediocrity	Spirit
Costa	Moving	Stuck
Crazy	Nonprofit	Talented
Dream	Opportunity	Town
Familiar	Potential	Valerie
Fullest	Power	Voice
Growth	Recognize	Volunteering

42   **Right at Home at Work**

Does your job match you? Do you match your job? Do you love it? Barely tolerate it? Hate it? Can't wait to get there?

Right work is a central tenet of many philosophies. But *being* right at work often gets overlooked. With so much of our time spent doing, being at, and thinking about work, don't we owe it to ourselves to place it at the core of our spiritual practice?

Work comes in many forms. Not all of them trade time for money. Whether we're sitting at a desk, changing diapers, weeding gardens, planning our next travel adventure, or doing yoga, we are working at something.

Think about your passions and hobbies. Who are you being when you're engaged in actions that bring you joy? Now think about who you are at work. Do these personas match? If not, how can you bring them more into alignment with your inner truth?

Being right at work means having the courage to express our genuine selves throughout the day. Do and be that and the right work will find you.

Practice bringing the best of yourself to whatever form of work you're engaged in. As this becomes a focus, the things we do for money naturally become more aligned with our passions. Work becomes a place where we feel increasingly more whole and fulfilled.

Who will you decide to be the next time you go to work? I hope it's your heart-centered, authentic self, engaged in a spirit-filled endeavor that lights up your soul.

—*Angelica Martinez*

Inspired Wisdom:

____ __ _ _____ ___ ____
_____ ____. ____ ____
____ ____

```
W A O R S R E P A I D K I S A
S T D A E E D G N I D E E W G
E F Z V A N G E L I C A O R Y
O U R E E P I A G A R D E N S
T S P I N N R U R A T R A E H
R S C S I I T A N U G R T U Y
A L E I N R T U C E O N U L O
I F E B T O O R R T G C E T J
M O N E Y N I V A E I P L Y H
A Y M K W L E S A M R C Y O S
O I S H I W P H S E R E E G O
T E O G O I U R T A D I N A U
D L H R R P A R T U P N G N L
E T K I L E V A R T A W E H I
S E T F U L F I L L E D L L T
```

Adventure	Gardens	Right
Angelica	Genuine	Soul
Authentic	Heart	Spirit
Best	Inner	Time
Courage	Joy	Travel
Desk	Lights	Truth
Diapers	Martinez	Weeding
Endeavor	Money	Whole
Engaged	Passions	Work
Fulfilled	Practice	Yoga

Center on Your Inner Wisdom

You are an eternal spirit, a unique aspect of the vast Oneness of all life.

Welcome your true, authentic, eternal self to be at home within your whole being. It's one of the most empowering experiences of life. Each moment becomes an adventure lived with love, confidence, courage, and increasing strength.

We can so easily forget who we really are. Life may then feel restricted and dull. When we remember to live centered with an open heart, life becomes hopeful, rich, and purposeful. Our eternal true self lies within our heart. It allows us to access our inner wisdom. Our body, emotions, mind, and soul are vehicles to manifest our deeply treasured true self in the world.

The circumstances of our life were planned by our eternal selves before we were born. They are the *workout machine of life* which strengthens our *soul muscles*. We improve our lives through personal empowerment.

These workouts make our unique gifts a little bit stronger each day through disciplined intention. We all still sometimes feel constrained, but restrictions are the power workout that build strength and endurance on the path to self-actualization.

Through dedicated inner exercise, our enhanced special qualities ground our exquisitely beautiful eternal spirit into daily life for the fulfillment of our true purpose. By cultivating our relationship with inner wisdom and living centered there, we increase confidence, trust, and inner strength. Stay aware and keep training. Get buff on the workout machine of life and pump up your soul muscles.

—*Eve Wilson*

Inspired Wisdom:

___ ___ ___   ___ ___ ___ ___ ___   ___ ___ ___ ___ ___ ___   ___ ___ ___ ___
___ ___ ___ ___   ___ ___ ___ ___ ___   ___ ___ ___ ___ ___ ___ ___   ___ ___ ___
___ ___ ___ ___   ___ ___   ___   ___ ___ ___ ___ ___   ___ ___ ___ ___ ___ ___   ___ ___ ___ ___
___ ___ ___

```
B C G I F T S L E H T I N N D
O O E E R N O I T N E T N I W
D U I N S D T O M G U A S I O
Y R P S T R E N G T H C R N D
D A E U U E Y C O T I U E T N
R G E S R M R V N P I N E R I
Y E T T T P H E L A E R E O M
U C G U H O O I D S R C I U T
A I N O D W N S S N N U S P D
E T E K D E S N E E O C D L S
T N O R D R P O D F L S A N A
L E V O L M I I U E U N L F E
E H F W U E F T S L R L I I E
L T L P E N H O P E F U L V W
B U F F O T D M T W I T E H J
O A H C I R Y E E V O R P M I
```

Authentic	Eternal	Oneness
Body	Eve	Pump
Buff	Gifts	Purposeful
Centered	Heart	Rich
Confidence	Hopeful	Soul
Courage	Improve	Spirit
Disciplined	Intention	Strength
Emotions	Love	Trust
Empowerment	Mind	Wilson
Endurance	Muscles	Workout

Let's Live Life

Let's live life.
One inside Oneness.
Open life's true vitality.
Let's live life
living calm and free inside.
Go past all hustle and bustle.
Let's come out and shine
from each cell of dark loneliness.
Let's open up and arise
from the closed doors of ego.
Rise up with heart
as all radiance of light.
Let's dissolve
from every loneliness.
Let's leave the darkness of suffocation
that just cannot breathe.
Let's laugh so very deeply and bright
with heart's rays shining love's happiness.
Silence comes for greening
all dried, yellow leaves.
Wounds of heart come healing too.
Self opens into every loving release.
Each binding chain is breaking free.
Arise now, living so very true.
One inside Oneness.
Let's live life!

—*Dr. Ram Sharma*

Inspired Wisdom:

_ _ _ _ _ _ _ _ _ _ _ _ _ _ _ _ _ _ _ _

_ _ _ _ _ _ _ _ _ _ _ _ _ _ _ _ _ _ _ _ _

_ _ _ _ _ _ _ _ _ _ _ _ _ _ _ _

```
E R T M R B L D R E V I L A C
S E R E H A E C N E L I S O N
H L U E U E D A V E N G E S S
I E E G P S A I R W D N I T H
N A H L H I T R A I G I N A N
E S Y A B A D L T N S N S S I
V E R E L U L I I F C E S N E
W M V I I T S L E A V E S H I
A J T L O Y A T A O N R N D E
C Y O N O E S C L I I G O U L
M L A C H S S D P E C E L L T
E E F I L M S P O N E N E S S
T H G I R B A I L I O P E N U
G E E R F H H R D T R A Y S H
```

Arise	Healing	Open
Bright	Heart	Radiance
Bustle	Hustle	Ram
Calm	Inside	Rays
Cell	Laugh	Release
Deeply	Leaves	Sharma
Dissolve	Life	Shine
Free	Live	Silence
Greening	Love	True
Happiness	Oneness	Vitality

45 Look Through Animal Eyes

Is there an animal in your environment, or a wild one in your yard? Look through their eyes for a moment. What do you see?

There is a difference between the way we look at the world and the way animals see things. Through human eyes, we look back at the past and wonder what might have been. We peer into the future, straining to see what will be. Animals, no matter the species, set their eyes upon the present and the reality that each moment has to offer, both good and bad.

Observing animals and walking with them in the present moment can remind us that there is grace and wisdom to be found even in simple, routine acts. Greeting a friend who has just come home with leaps and woofs of joy and enthusiasm says "I love you," and perhaps "Can I have a cookie?"

A feline's entreaty to join her in a sunbeam nap offers the experience of precious serenity, as well as priceless companionship. Focusing on the present can offer us insight into forgiveness and the putting-behind of past transgressions.

With an acceptance of the now, we are free to forgive and start again within ourselves. We create our relationships, both with animals and humans in the present, leaving the past and future behind.

Animals are not looking for perfection in us, or in themselves. They seek out the true intention of the heart, beyond words and deeds. Animals teach us that unconditional love overrides judgement and opens the door to new possibilities within us all.

—*Lauren McCall*

Inspired Wisdom:

_____ _____ __ ____ ___
_____ _____ ___
_____ __ ___ _____ _____

```
W  L  L  A  C  C  M  G  S  E  I  C  E  P  S
W  I  A  N  I  E  M  A  R  L  S  S  E  R  E
O  V  S  A  C  C  E  P  T  A  N  C  E  E  I
O  E  A  D  S  W  N  S  I  S  C  E  Y  A  K
F  T  N  N  O  I  T  C  E  F  R  E  P  N  O
S  H  D  O  W  M  H  S  O  F  S  N  D  P  O
E  G  R  I  W  F  U  U  L  O  T  E  R  A  C
C  I  H  T  T  N  S  Y  F  R  I  E  N  D  E
H  S  R  N  B  R  I  S  T  G  C  A  N  S  F
U  N  N  E  R  U  A  L  D  I  G  U  L  I  E
M  I  A  T  D  D  S  E  O  V  N  A  E  S  L
A  M  S  N  L  I  M  U  H  E  M  E  P  N  I
N  O  U  I  R  D  S  A  I  I  L  A  R  Y  N
S  L  W  P  R  E  S  E  N  T  E  I  V  E  E
N  A  P  E  Y  O  J  A  S  L  L  O  V  E  S
```

Acceptance	Humans	Perfection
Animals	Insight	Precious
Cookie	Intention	Present
Enthusiasm	Joy	See
Eyes	Lauren	Serenity
Feline	Leaps	Species
Forgive	Love	Sunbeam
Friend	McCall	Wild
Grace	Nap	Wisdom
Heart	Now	Woofs

Connection

Every human, animal, and plant on the planet requires connection. We are lost without it. Our very survival depends on it.

As humans, our need to belong to something bigger than us is part of our spiritual purpose. It's the way we find fulfillment. Animals create balance in the human and planetary ecosystem. Domesticated animal family members help us experience unconditional love. The plant kingdom provides us with air, food, and medicine.

Our world is abundant with connection. Yet so many times we feel lost and alone on our journey through life. We feel isolated and like we don't belong. We lose sight of who we are and why we are here. Our bodies, our health, and our happiness are weakened when starved of connection.

There are many simple ways to reconnect. Get outside. Go for a walk. Smile and say "Hi" to a stranger. Take a moment. Feel connected.

Nature's silent beauty and healing is always there, patiently waiting to relate with each of us. It is in our connection that we find solutions, guidance, beauty, and love. The natural world provides us with a plethora of examples on how connection, cooperation, and compassion lead to a happy, abundant life.

Reach out and touch someone today. Talk to your plants. Notice the squirrel in the park. Pat your beloved animal companion. Smell the flowers. Feel the grass between your toes. Notice that you are part and parcel of it all. Isn't that wonderful? Feel the exquisite joy of connection.

—*Teresa Helgeson*

Inspired Wisdom:

‗ ‗ ‗ ‗ ‗   ‗ ‗ ‗   ‗ ‗   ‗ ‗ ‗ ‗ ‗ ‗   ‗ ‗   ‗

‗ ‗ ‗ ‗ ‗ ‗ ‗ ‗ ‗ ‗ ‗ ‗   ‗ ‗ ‗   ‗ ‗ ‗ ‗ ‗ ‗

‗ ‗ ‗   ‗ ‗ ‗ ‗ ‗ ‗ ‗ ‗ ‗

```
C O N N E C T I O N F G B P E
T O U C H H T N I L F R N L K
G O O U A T O N O I U A N A L
P U R P O S E W E N L S A N A
T U P R E E E I S L F S A T W
P Y R G E R L E R R I U Q S W
B S L C S Y A R I N L S T O P
T E I N T O S T O N L F N P L
H O L U O L E I I T M D A L A
R E A O A I S C E O E H D A U
S E A M V S N R N R N E N N T
B M I L A E E A F A T A U E I
L N I P I S D U P S D T B T R
A H M L A N L L E M S I A A I
N O D H E A G O P P O I U N P
C E S S M E T S Y S O C E G S
```

Abundant	Fulfillment	Smell
Animals	Grass	Smile
Beauty	Guidance	Spiritual
Beloved	Happy	Squirrel
Companion	Healing	Teresa
Compassion	Helgeson	Toes
Connection	Planet	Touch
Cooperation	Plants	Walk
Ecosystem	Purpose	Wonderful
Flowers	Silent	

Ode to Mother Earth

Reverently inspired by Psalm 23.

The Earth is my shelter, I shall not want.
I lean on Her green pastures as
She speaks through quiet waters that restore my soul.
She shows me the high road that serves all.
And even though I walk through the valley of the shadow of stress,
I fear no upheaval, for She is always there to rest upon.

Mother Earth is infinite in wisdom. She is an ancient living library adapting the old and creating new life. Her wisdom follows the path of least resistance. Observing her can be our greatest teacher: physically, emotionally, and spiritually. Her endless generosity spins infinite webs of collaborative counterpoint. Her resilient workings are both seen and unseen, and perfectly tuned for renewal. She plays in the springtime, works all summer, sheds abundantly in the fall, and rests in the winter. She models the rhythms of regeneration for us.

My fear is not believable when I am with You, Mother.
Your sod and your tree, they comfort me.
You prepare a feast before me in the presence of what is,
right before my eyes.
You wash my head with rain as your brother, the sky,
overflows like your abundance.
Goodness and grace, they flow from You all the days of my life.
And in your comfort I will dwell now and forever more.

—*Dr. Paul Rudy*

Inspired Wisdom:

__ __ __ __ __ __ __ __ __ __ __ __ __ __ __
__ __ __ __ __ __ __ __ __ __ __ __
__ __ __ __ __ __ __

```
C O R E M M U S H E L T E R P
R N L P A U L L L S C A W E S
H I B L S S E N D O O G E T A
Y A P O A F R R G A L D B I L
T R T A E F I E C R L O S N M
H N Y A S G L O H W A I T I H
M M S T N T M I E T B C O F T
S T H I I F U C B A O E E N R
E P V L O S N R N R R M A I R
T I R R A A O C E E A Y D U R
L H T I D W I R H S T R L E E
O D E N N E E C E A I D Y S T
T O U O N G A N U N V R R E N
S B T T O E P R E S E N C E I
A E A R T H R A T R I G O N W
```

Abundance	Infinite	Renewal
Ancient	Library	Rhythms
Collaborative	Living	Rudy
Comfort	Mother	Shelter
Earth	Ode	Sod
Fall	Paul	Spring
Feast	Pastures	Summer
Generosity	Presence	Teacher
Goodness	Psalm	Webs
Grace	Rain	Winter

Food Wisdom for All

In the twentieth century, food went from being a nurturing part of everyday experience to a commodity to be marketed. *This food will make you more beautiful and look younger. That food will make you healthier and feel more vibrant.*

Today, many people look to food as a source of entertainment. This distancing from the natural purpose of food has led to all kinds of eating problems and disorders and unrealistic expectations. Weight management is a huge industry.

In ancient times, the majority of people foraged, harvested, or killed their own food. Eating and preparing food was a communal activity, as eating alone was not a sustainable practice. This is the first time in history that humans have practiced solitary eating and live at such a great distance from the earthly source of their nutrition.

When we stop requiring that our food be super or perfectly pure, we can experience the daily grounding in our bodies that the nourishing act of eating is meant to provide. The anxiety that so many of us feel around what to eat can be healed when we remember the sacred purpose of food.

These insights were provided courtesy of Ceres, the grain goddess of ancient Rome. Her name is the root word for *cereal*. Ceres can guide you into an appropriate relationship with food. She says to let go of your anxiety about eating right, and to stop beating yourself up over your food choices.

Ceres asks you to practice gratitude every time you eat, no matter what you eat, as a reminder that the Earth sustains you.

Bon appétit!

—Thea Wirsching

Inspired Wisdom:

___ ___ ___   ___ ___ ___ ___ ___ ___   ___ ___ ___ ___ ___ ___   ___ ___   ___ ___ ___ ___

___ ___   ___ ___ ___ ___ ___   ___ ___ ___ ___ ___ ___ ___   ___ ___ ___ ___   ___ ___ ___

___ ___ ___ ___ ___ ___ ___ ___ ___   ___ ___   ___ ___ ___   ___ ___ ___ ___ ___

```
E L T T H P R E P A R I N G E
D A I E M O R O O T S A H R C
I R T L L S E C I O H C E A R
U U E I A B N E D P U L A T R
G T P B N E A I P O A E L I S
E A P O M G R N A T H F E T F
O N A G O E D E I T I S D U D
W L A N U M M O C A S S N D A
I I L I Y C N E Y E T U O E N
T A R H C S T S R H T S S W I
T H T S H E E E G R W H U E A
B U N I C T C I I I D F A S N
C E P R R H S T S E I D O B O
F T U U G N I D N U O R G O H
E O O O I O O N I A R G E A D
S C R N N M T H G O D D E S S
```

Appetit	Grain	Relationship
Bodies	Gratitude	Remember
Cereal	Grounding	Rome
Ceres	Guide	Root
Choices	Healed	Source
Communal	Insights	Sustainable
Courtesy	Natural	Sustains
Eating	Nourishing	Thea
Food	Nutrition	Wirsching
Goddess	Preparing	Wisdom

Beauty

What is beauty? We often think of it as something we see with our eyes. From nature and color, to food and artwork. A field of sunflowers. A plate of colorful French macarons. A sunset at the beach. A snowy mountaintop. We say, "Wow, that's beautiful!"

And then, of course, there are people. We've all seen people that we would describe as having great beauty. Their features stir something within us. We automatically think, "They are really beautiful!"

Yet visual aesthetics are only one type of beauty. There is also beauty that can be heard. Beautiful music. Beautiful poetry. The beautiful sounds of nature.

There is also a much deeper form of beauty that cannot be seen and cannot be heard. This type of beauty is something we feel. Feelings can be beautiful. Love, for example, is a beautiful thing to feel. Love is beauty. Whether it is love for a person, a pet, a job, a hobby, or a way of living your life. Love is beautiful.

For a person, there is also inner beauty. This is something that comes from within. It is who they are as a person. Their kindness, their honesty, their sincerity, their compassion, their goodness. Inner beauty shines the brightest of all.

The beauty that is you as a person is more of a standout than the beauty that shows on the outside.

—*Taylor Wansley*

Inspired Wisdom:

___ _____ _____ ___

_____ ___ _____ __

___

```
R O L O C R O L Y A T T L E
E H F S N O R A C A M E D Y
N S R E B L M E A E E I W N
N U E U T U Y P D F S O A W
I N N R I F C I A N N T T H
I S C N U I S V I S U A L G
Y E H O S T U S I R S H I O
W T N U U U A N E E L I H O
E A M O S A C E T P H O O D
K I N D N E S S F E N E V N
B R I S R B G P O E T R Y E
H T E I L P S T S D O O F S
O F T A L E E T S D N U O S
L Y H O B B Y T U A E B O J
```

Beautiful	Hobby	Outside
Beauty	Honesty	Pet
Color	Inner	Poetry
Compassion	Inside	Sincerity
Deeper	Job	Snowy
Features	Kindness	Sounds
Feel	Love	Sunset
Food	Macarons	Taylor
French	Music	Visual
Goodness	Nature	Wansley

50 Zen and the Blossom

Living in Japan, the concepts of Buddhism and Zen are everywhere. There are constant reminders of deference to elders. It's important to have your own *wa* or balance in order. Clarity of mind and respect for others' space are essential. It's not a club to join but rather something that you reflect upon in your own time and space. No competition.

In Japanese culture, the coming of spring and the blossoming trees are a great excuse to join together and celebrate the season. Friends meet and eat under the spectacular groves of pink canopy. It is called *hanami* and is the epitome of the essence of beauty and community.

As photographers attempting to capture these beautiful ephemeral moments, we all want to create masterpieces, not snapshots. To discover this secret of seeing, walk around and take the scene in before shooting. Distill the essence of what you see. Frame your vision. No cropping necessary.

Creating lasting images of cherry blossoms or any of life's precious seconds with a photo or brain/memory slides is an act of losing oneself. It's like the art of Zen. Free the mind of thought, disappear into the scent, and surround yourself in the perfect beauty of now. Focus on the *elements*, but as a complete picture.

And then, just as in life, it's gone. The season is short. The factors that make it a great challenge to photograph are the same that make it disappear. The sun or lack of it, the wind that makes the trees and limbs dance, and the rain which nourishes but also washes away the last of the petals.

Watching the blossoms float away as a gust of wind takes them on pink snowy flight is pure joy.

—*Paul Diserio*

Inspired Wisdom:

_ _ _ _ _ _ _ _   _ _ _   _ _ _ _ _   _ _ _ _ _

_ _ _ _ _ _ _   _ _ _ _ _ _ _   _ _ _ _

_ _ _ _ _ _ _   _ _ _   _ _   _ _ _

```
C A Y R R E H C S T E R C E S
P M T G U R S N L P E N A N C
D A S R A B O L H A E V G O E
R S H O E W L E A Z R A N R N
T T W V Y A M O Y T O I I R E
M E L E M E N T S I E C T S E
I R N S R G U E R S A P E Y R
P P M A D A S E C N O E E O U
M I L E E A S R O N I M L N T
T E N B J I N P E N E S F T C
L C T K D A Y C G D H S A A I
U E T I M M P E E R L O S S P
A S T O H S P A N S L E E E Y
P O U I N A J O N F E M A R F
H A N A M I W R E F L E C T Y
```

Beauty	Essence	Picture
Blossom	Fleeting	Pink
Canopy	Float	Reflect
Cherry	Frame	Scene
Clarity	Groves	Secret
Dance	Hanami	Seeing
Diserio	Japan	Snapshots
Elders	Masterpieces	Snowy
Elements	Paul	Wa
Ephemeral	Petals	Zen

The Power of Prayer

Do you believe in the power of prayer? Research has repeatedly shown it's real. Many of us have been inspired to pray for, hold loving space for, or send energy to others and situations as a way to help each other. Have you ever wondered if your prayers, good wishes, kind thoughts, and best intentions had any real, measurable, and noticeable impact on a situation?

> Prayer, prayer always changes reality, let us not forget that. It either changes things or changes our hearts, but it always changes.
> —Pope Francis

A powerful example of the power of prayer is that of Alex Trebek, television's longtime beloved host of *Jeopardy!* In March of 2019, he announced he was diagnosed with stage-four pancreatic cancer. Within days, at least a million people sent him emails, cards, text messages, and tweets wishing him well. His well-wishers were praying for him and sending him positive energy. After just two months, and with expert chemotherapy, Trebek reported that the cancer was in "near remission." According to his doctors, this positive dramatic change was almost unheard of.

In addition to his excellent medical team, Trebek credits, in *People Magazine*, the outpouring of positive support from fans all over for the success of his treatment. His doctors agreed.

Contributing author Janette Stuart is another traveler on the journey through cancer. She says:

> So many people are supporting me in the most important of ways by sending love and light and healing prayers my way. I have people that pray for me daily, and I can feel the love. People really do want to help and asking for their support in this way is a benefit to the giver and receiver.

So how do prayer and loving intention work?

> Prayer is as real as the force of gravity. It can reach a realm where reason is too feeble to enter. It can work miracles. Its magnanimous efficacy is indescribable. Its potency can be hardly comprehended without actual experience.—Swami Sivananda

Some of us approach life from the spiritual perspective that God by every name we call Him (Her/Them/It) is in some way omnipresent and/or omnipotent. Others prefer the more scientific approach of oneness, resonance, and the unified field, and that we are all connected through subtle energies. Regardless of our particular persuasion, most of us can agree that our loving intentions that some call prayer travel beyond time and space. They can be received by others. Do they go to another realm? Is it Divine? Is it potential? Each person must answer these questions for themselves, or even whether the questions are valid. Belief systems vary. May the Force be with you.

> The oneness just means one thing...that the oneness, beyond space and time, is another domain of reality.... The oneness is causally potent because this oneness chooses out of the potentiality what becomes actuality. —Dr. Amit Goswami, quantum physicist

No matter how we perceive it, our lives are influenced by our intentions. In intention, the individual is the creator. In prayer, the Divine field cocreates by responding to a direct communication from the individual in words and feelings. Both work.

> In the beginning was the Word, and the Word was with God, and the Word was God. —John 1:1

When someone prays for us or sends loving energy to us, we are able to receive the love because it is sent to our energetic home address which has a specific, unique frequency. It's like how our devices and computers receive and send information, or how we can tune into a radio station for our favorite music.

What can you do when you feel like you want help? Pray or send love. The exact words of what you call it don't matter. We're talking energy here. Say what resonates with you and your belief system. It's powerful. It makes a difference. You make a difference.

What's the best way to pray/send love? Whatever feels right to you. If you're experienced with prayer, or beaming, or whatever you call it, use that. Want to experiment with a different form? Here's a simple method that many find works.

Close your eyes. Put your hand over your heart. (Are you still breathing through your nose?)

Notice the beat of your heart. Inhale. Exhale. (This may feel stupid but give it a chance.) Inhale. Exhale. Notice the beat of your heart.

Send love from your heart to a situation or a person with no opinion or expectation of what the outcome will be. Give space for God/the Universe/the Potentiality to have a better idea/the perfect solution/answer. Say *please* and *thank you* as you commune. Open your eyes when done.

Our positive intentions and loving prayers matter. Energy flows where attention goes. Our thoughts, words, and deeds matter. You matter. What you do matters. Who you are matters. We all matter.

As we intertwine our energy fields with love, caring, and compassion, we not only make a difference in others' lives and help out our friends and loved ones but also make a difference in our own.

Sending you kind intentions of much love and many blessings. Thank you for being you!

51 **A Letter to You from Santa**

Dear boys and girls of all ages,

Santa here. I wanted to return to you some of the love you've given me over the years. No matter if you believe in me or not, I believe in you. Santa is a twinkle in the eye, an expression of joy and delight, and we all need more of that.

Follow your dreams, and go where your heart leads you. Make time for people you love and care about. Presence means so much more than presents. Spread joy and hope and love around. What you give may be way more important than what you receive.

We all have that special space within that is our inner Santa. No red suit or specific belief system necessary. We can access our inner Santa any time we want by what we choose to think about and focus on and how we treat the people in our world. Santa listens to kids of all ages with patience and tolerance. We hear their hopes, their dreams, and their wishes. Santa takes it all in without judgement and does what he can to make it real.

Make love your legacy. I sure do, and I believe in you. I believe in your ability to bring joy into lives wherever you go. I'll help you to believe in the real magic of life and love, which is family and friends and the spirit of the moment.

Spread the seeds of hope and possibility far and wide, and be there for the folks you love when they need you. Your legacy of love will be a present that just keeps on giving.

Merry Christmas spirit all year!

With love from,

—*Santa Loren Smith*

Inspired Wisdom:

___ _____ _____ ___
____ ___ ____ _____ ___
_____

```
T H H E L G R T E S A F T E A
Y R R E M O W S D G I R L S T
M P T G A I R I I J F I T S N
Y A O U N R K E O S D E S P A
G T G K E I T Y N P E N A R S
V I L I E V A R E I L D M E E
L E G A C Y E C G R I S T S L
O N V E R L N I C I G Y S E A
U C G E S A V A L T H O I N S
H E N E R I R O T E T B R T M
E N P E N E V R A N B D H L I
I O L G I E D R E A M S C S T
H O T E E C N E S E R P N I H
T W I S H E S F A M I L Y N G
```

Believe	Heart	Patience
Boys	Hopes	Presence
Care	Inner	Present
Christmas	Joy	Santa
Delight	Kids	Smith
Dreams	Legacy	Spirit
Family	Loren	Tolerance
Friends	Love	Twinkle
Girls	Magic	Wishes
Giving	Merry	

The Power of Love

52

Love is the most powerful, magnetic, and attractive force in the universe. It's a force that resides as pure, powerful energy within each of us. Activate this energy to experience more loving and healthier relationships, inner peace, radiant and vibrant health, abundant wealth, and whatever your pure heart desires.

Love is a force we can feel and use but cannot touch. It comes from within. It increases our capacity to be more of the marvelous being that we are. Love is absolute energy of good. That's why when we are in love, we do good things for ourselves and others. It's felt all around us. The impact of love is measurable yet goes way beyond what is quantifiable.

Society misconstrues the meaning of love. It is thought of as an emotion. This is only partly right, as emotions are simply energy in motion. Many believe love is something someone gives you. That means it can be taken away. The truth is we are born in love; love is the truth of our beings. The experience of love is simply its activation from within. Being grateful for all love enhances life and experience.

Tap into the vibration of love. Make the greatest contribution you can make to yourself, each other, and the planet. Enter into the heart field of pure creative potential where the powerful energy of love manifests and multiplies.

Take the shackles off of love. Feel your heart expand and revel in the sweetness. Let love circulate in and around and through you. Embrace and experience the power of love.

—*Dr. Wendy Mears-Kaveney*

Inspired Wisdom:

— — — — — — — — — — — — — — — — — — —

— — — — — — — — — — — — — — —

— — — — — — — — — — — — — — — — — — — — —

```
R M E V E U N I V E R S E R L
A E A Y T P H I N H N G I S O
D R P N O L A I T N E T O P V
I U O W I S S L I B E L V E E
A P E W H F A L E V E R I E M
N R N S W E E T N E S S B A W
T S E E W M A S G H E A R T C
C E V I T C A R T T A V A C R
E I S S A A A G N S E D T A E
C L Y T Y T L E N L I N I V A
M P A D E H C U O E A T O Y T
E I E F N A T U C D T T N G I
A T U H E E S L N R E I O R V
R L F P V O W U A R I O C E E
S U T N A R B I V E D C C N E
O M F L K A T R U T H O V E E
```

Abundant	Kaveney	Pure
Attractive	Love	Radiant
Circulate	Magnetic	Revel
Creative	Manifests	Sweetness
Energy	Marvelous	Truth
Good	Mears	Universe
Grateful	Multiplies	Vibrant
Health	Peace	Vibration
Heart	Potential	Wealth
Inner	Power	Wendy

53   **Believe in Magic**

Do you believe in magic? Belief is a funny thing. It impacts us in strange and extraordinary ways. What we believe in and focus on tends to appear in our lives, be it good, bad, or indifferent.

What do you focus on? Consider being someone who doesn't fixate on the negativity, stress, and angst out in the world. We each have the power to choose what we give our attention to and how we respond to it.

Magic doesn't have to be all about rainbows, dragons, mermaids, unicorns, or rabbits out of hats. It can be about being moved to tears by exquisite tenderness and kindness. The sublime beauty of nature. That cherished special smile dawning on a loved one's face. Savoring a quiet moment of peace in your heart.

Check it out. Look for magic in your day today. Make a game of it. See it peeping out when you celebrate getting the perfect parking spot or catch it in the enchanting shape of a cloud. Notice those pennies on the ground. Are they from heaven? Is someone saying hello, or sending you a hug? Enjoy that special moment.

Need help? Kids are great at spotting and discovering magic.

Want more happiness in your life? Cultivate magic, or kindness, or compassion, or anything you choose and rediscover wonder. Looking for it, we see it more. Make it a mindfulness practice. Does it show up more because we create it? Or was it always there and we're just now noticing? Don't know. Isn't that magic?

—Melissa Morgan

Inspired Wisdom:

_ _ _ _ _ _ _ _ _ _   _ _ _ _ _

_ _ _ _ _ _ _   _ _ _   _ _ _   _ _ _ _ _ _ _   _ _

_ _ _ _

```
E C A E P O W E R M A N I F S
L C I E H S T E R U T A N M U
I H I G E E V E I L E B I N C
M E R M A I D S A Y N N U F O
S R N G R M S S E N D N I K F
M I A C T A S G L F E G S I C
C S G R H I P A U T R N E E N
S H R A L A I L A S N I I S E
T E O E R C N V T W E P N N V
R D M K E E I T E O S E N O A
A S I P S T J O I B S E E G E
N N S S L Y S S E N I P P A H
G A S U B L I M E I G N D R D
E E C L S T I B B A R I G D H
T I N L U N I C O R N S I F E
```

Believe	Kindness	Pennies
Cherished	Magic	Power
Cultivate	Melissa	Rabbits
Dragons	Mermaids	Rainbows
Enchanting	Mindfulness	Smile
Focus	Morgan	Special
Funny	Nature	Strange
Happiness	Parking	Sublime
Heart	Peace	Tenderness
Heaven	Peeping	Unicorns

Soul Identity

We are magical beings. We are here for a sacred purpose. We are multidimensional souls. We have traveled through the universe to be here now. We are full of soul gifts. Expression is waiting to burst out of us. We are ripe and ready for big changes. The soul is calling us to push through our blocks. The prize is to witness the blast of our own soul light.

What is your secret soul identity?

You are a massive gift to humanity. Your soul light is magnificent. It is a ray weaving in the expanding tapestry of life. You are here for a reason. Who are you really? What do you uniquely have to offer this planet and this time?

The cells in our body change because of environmental signals. So do we. We change our state of being according to input from our environment. The input received depends on what we are open to. When we shift our identity, we shift our reality. We can embody change within ourselves and the world.

Now is the time we have been waiting for. Explore and share your secret soul identity. Allow your unique brilliance to be revealed.

—*Alessandra Gilioli*

Inspired Wisdom:

__ ____ ___ _____ _____

__ _____ _ _____

_____ __ ____ ___ ___

_____

```
A M A G N I F I C E N T W E H
L A V E T E B H E E S P O W R
L A E R Z W R V I Y D O B M E
O T L I H I I N R T S U U A
W O R E I S L G N I I T N L S
T P E A S F L R G T P I F N O
I E Y A Q S I N U N V E E I N
L S M R H S A C R E D P P E G
O N S I T L N N R D O C U Y R
I E F E S S C S D I V O R L T
L T U P N I E U E R O L P X E
I I O O T N P O F A L O O R
G V W E F O I R A B L A S T C
M A G I C A L W T T H E E W E
O T H G I L R C E L L S L D S
```

Alessandra	Input	Ripe
Allow	Light	Sacred
Blast	Magical	Secret
Brilliance	Magnificent	Shift
Cells	Massive	Signals
Embody	Now	Soul
Explore	Open	Tapestry
Gifts	Prize	Universe
Gilioli	Purpose	Witness
Identity	Reason	

Tell Your Story

Every time we tell our story, we create our reality. Our lives are what we tell them to be.

Have you ever heard a magician say "Abracadabra"? The phrase comes from Hebrew or Aramaic and means *it will be created as I speak*. We create as we speak. Every time we use language, we weave a web of perception. These are the webs that connect us to the reality around us.

Tell your story in the same way a spider weaves her web. Attract life experiences by telling the stories that you want. Let your stories glisten in the moonlight and draw in the life that sustains you.

What life experience do you want? If it is love, tell your life as a love story. If you want to be an artist, tell the story of your creative responses to everything. If you want to be a wise person, unlock your awareness of the fullness of your soul's wisdom by telling its story.

You have infinite power to create your world as you speak. Grab hold of it! You can start by telling your story to a journal, to a friend, or to strangers. Offer the gift of your perception to yourself and those around you. Learn to listen to the stories of others. Soon you will be enmeshed in a web much larger than yourself. Your story will hold limitless possibility. Tell yourself a tale of joy and delight. Or transformation. It's your story. What do you want it to be?

—*Amalia Scott*

Inspired Wisdom:

____ ____ _____ __ ___

____ __ ___ __ _____ __

___ _____ ____ ____

```
T W E R B E H E P R E W O P G
K N O W I N G N E S S J R L L
L Y O S B E W G R O U E O R I
M A G I C I A N C S D E T Y S
J O O R T U Y R E I A T W D T
O E O S G A E Y P O U I O E E
U V W N A A M S T G S N R H N
R O A N L T T R I D I I D S O
N L S I E I C E O I T F U E N
A F T O L I G M N F L N T M T
L Y E D A A A H S Y S I O N T
U C L M R E M A T T E N Y E O
O U A R B A D A C A R B A R C
A R T I S T L S P E A K I R S
A L U O S T H G I L E D F E T
```

Abracadabra	Journal	Scott
Amalia	Joy	Soul
Aramaic	Knowingness	Speak
Artist	Language	Spider
Delight	Love	Tale
Enmeshed	Magician	Transformation
Gift	Moonlight	Webs
Glisten	Perception	Wisdom
Hebrew	Power	Word
Infinite	Reality	

56 Internal Authority

Life, thankfully, has no one right answer. We all approach it a little differently.

That means that we get to create the meaning of our own existence. How cool is that? Defining our own meaning is an incredibly empowering experience. We can choose to embark on affirming and positive pathways of thought. We can lend our energy to uplifting ideas, which will energize us in return.

Consider beauty, success, intelligence, and progress. These are concepts we often use to judge or measure ourselves. You are the author of your own story. You have control of your inner universe. Beauty can be anything for you. Expand its significance to include yourself. You can redefine success so that you celebrate every small achievement. Hold yourself not to the standards of others, but to your own personal ethics and authority.

Authority works best if we are flexible. Open yourself to change, growth, challenges, healthy failure, and uncertainty. No matter what happens, it's all part of your meaningful story and fulfilling journey. Our quest here is to learn and grow.

Have fun with it! Realize your freedom. Create with love and compassion. Your unique take on life is a precious resource for yourself and those around you. Just as you are inspired by the outlook of others, humanity is all the more vibrant when you add your story to the multitude. Collectively we rise.

—*Kaley Elizabeth Oliver*

Inspired Wisdom:

_ __ _____

_____ _ _____ ___ ____

_____ _____

_____

```
I  A  T  S  U  O  I  C  E  R  P  M  C  O  N
Y  T  S  I  N  U  L  D  A  L  L  Y  C  H  R
R  T  E  R  E  E  U  E  S  C  I  H  T  E  U
O  A  U  P  A  T  H  W  A  Y  S  E  W  V  N
T  T  Q  A  I  A  I  N  G  R  B  S  G  I  I
S  I  N  T  E  R  N  A  L  A  N  A  N  T  Q
K  A  L  E  Y  B  V  I  Z  A  B  T  I  I  U
R  U  A  F  L  E  X  I  B  L  E  N  T  S  E
M  T  G  N  I  L  L  I  F  L  U  F  F  O  I
T  H  A  N  R  E  V  I  L  O  D  E  I  P  N
C  O  L  L  E  C  T  I  V  E  L  Y  L  M  N
P  R  S  S  E  R  G  O  R  P  O  W  P  E  E
R  I  I  N  R  E  S  O  U  R  C  E  U  G  R
I  T  N  G  N  I  N  A  E  M  B  A  R  K  T
E  Y  R  C  N  A  L  S  U  C  C  E  S  S  W
F  R  E  E  D  O  M  O  W  O  R  G  R  L  D
```

Answer	Fulfilling	Pathways
Authority	Grow	Positive
Beauty	Inner	Precious
Celebrate	Intelligence	Progress
Collectively	Internal	Quest
Elizabeth	Kaley	Resource
Embark	Learn	Story
Ethics	Meaning	Success
Flexible	Multitude	Unique
Freedom	Oliver	Uplifting

57 **Some Words of Wisdom**

These are some of the gems I've mined from my life.

Be kind. Be patient with others and with yourself.

Find the endeavors that bring you joy, and seek out ways to make a living from those. When we follow our passions in our work, we embrace our lives enthusiastically. This makes a career, or careers, a lifelong journey.

An orderly life is an empty canvas on which to create. Our living and working spaces are part of the artist's palette that gives us scope for creating new beauty. At the end of the day, time is our most precious commodity. Organization of time includes meeting obligations, keeping engagements, and allowing unstructured time to explore and imagine.

Procrastination, just as much as worry, is the thief of time. If something undone weighs on your mind, just do it. Then move on to something new and interesting.

Encourage others in their quests and nourish their dreams when you can. Allow time for your own dreams and quests. Above all, be kind.

—*Simon Spalding*

Inspired Wisdom:

_ _ _ _ _ _ _ _ _ _ _ _ _ _ _ _

_ _ _ _ _ _ _ _ _ _ _ _ _ _ _ _ _ _ _ _ _

_ _ _ _ _ _

```
N Y S I G W P G E R O L P X E
M O L E O A C O N E P O C S C
N S M R T R A Y N I S L S O A
V S D I E E O D N E D M A Y N
E S E A S D E M I T A L T N V
O N T E C A R B M E H U A T A
T E C J V T H O R S A S S P S
E E R O O C A D I E U E N M S
T N R U U Y A R B O U Y O O E
T S W R K R U R I Q D T I D F
E T O N I O A C E H E P S S I
L R R E N E E G S E T M S I L
A W K Y D R I L E L R E A W F
P O L L P I M A G I N E P O W
```

Beauty	Gems	Patient
Canvas	Imagine	Precious
Career	Journey	Quest
Create	Joy	Simon
Dreams	Kind	Scope
Embrace	Life	Spalding
Empty	Nourish	Time
Encourage	Orderly	Wisdom
Endeavors	Palette	Words
Explore	Passions	Work

58   **We Can Change the World**

"Changing the world" is a phrase often associated with powerful politicians, roaring activists, or far-off fantasies. The reality is that we can all be agents of change.

Climate change seems to be a huge, global issue that someone else will take care of. The truth is that preserving the environment is a responsibility that belongs to each and every one of us.

In spite of all of our differences and diversity, the human race has one prevailing similarity: the planet on which we live. We must protect our miraculous home. We are all tiny yet mighty forces. By working together toward one common goal, we will slowly but surely be chipping away at the massive problems ahead of us.

What can we do? Acknowledge the fact that our planet is in danger. It's the first step in contributing to positive, lasting change. Get educated. Make your life an example.

Reduce usage of single-use plastics and other disposable items. Reuse water bottles, food containers, and grocery bags. Properly recycle all items possible. Shop locally. Donate what you are done with rather than throwing it away. Eat less red meat. Use fewer fossil fuels. Turn off the water while brushing your teeth. Just with these actions, we can all make seemingly small but surprisingly overwhelming contributions to preserve the environment.

Climate change looms over all of us as an impending global crisis. Expecting others to fix it won't work. It may seem like a trek up a steep mountainside, but the only way to do it is to work together and just start climbing.

Every day in every way, change begins with you and me.

—*Gigi Accomazzo*

Inspired Wisdom:

— — — — — — — — — — — — — — — —

— — — — — — — — — — — — — — — — —

— — — — — — — — — — — — — — — — —

```
S T E E P L A N E T Y H E A
R E G N A H C F T A T N D E
E A F B R A T O H A H R N V
E F O S P E C R L L G V H R
O L S U O L U C A R I M T E
G E D W I D T E O R M H E S
N T E H O C Y S O M E S E E
A I X N O N E N M L A Y T R
E L A M I W M L R L L Z E P
T T M T O E A E C L A A Z T
E O P R N G D R A Y K O M O
N E L T E U E C I R C E G S
S D E N C T O G E T H E R F
O R T E A L I M E S U E R T
A S R W E G A S E M O H O N
```

Accomazzo	Goal	Reduce
Agents	Home	Reuse
Change	Locally	Small
Common	Mighty	Steep
Donate	Miraculous	Teeth
Environment	Mountain	Tiny
Example	Off	Together
Forces	Planet	Trek
Gigi	Preserve	Water
Global	Recycle	World

59   Givers Receive the Most

Life is about creating yourself. Who do you want to be? How about a charitable superhero?

When you impact the life of another through volunteering, be it companionship, soothing comfort, positive energy, financial support, or time, it provides deep fulfillment and valuable satisfaction. You become an integral part of changing lives.

Altruism through volunteering is pure human kindness with an internal thermometer for joy. Our service raises the level of consciousness all around. We enrich our lives and communities. That old saying "It is in giving that we receive" is true.

Neuroscience shows that giving is a powerful pathway for creating more personal joy and improving overall health. It encourages the brain to release the feel-good happiness trifecta of the neurochemicals dopamine, serotonin, and oxytocin into our bodies.

Being an example of selfless compassion trickles down to others. Gratitude continues and encourages the goodwill-kindness chain. What a wonderful thing to be part of.

When passionate generosity is intrinsically motivated and positively focused, the whole world benefits. We impact lives. Everyone blossoms in this environment of giving.

In turn, we have more abundance for the creation of peace and unity for the planet. As we transform our soulful, heartfelt compassion through generous, charitable giving, we cultivate deeper relationships of mind, body, and spirit. Every bit of this helps in the healing of humanity.

Being proactive and spiritually giving awakens a huge surge of love, happiness, and belonging. This matters. Reach out. Volunteer. Offer yourself and reap unlimited rewards.

—*René Stern*

Inspired Wisdom:

— — — — — — — — — — — — — — — — — —

— — — — — — — — — — — — — — — — — — — —

— — — — — — — — — — — — —

```
O S E R V O L U N T E E R V I
X C E E B X A C O M F O R T L
Y E R E N E L B A T I R A H C
T T V K B P L S R E V I G S O
O U S I A E G O O D W I L L M
C E N N E A N R N R E T S G P
I V C D D C H E E G L P R S A
N I Y N M E E H F S I A A G S
H T T E A K E R S I T N E N S
E C I S H D E E U I T V G I I
A A N S M W N P T A O S N H O
L O U I A I L U F L U O S T N
I R T R P Y D S B A N D O O U
N P D P R E N I M A P O D O W
G S A T C E F I R T O R L S D
W H H O L S E R O T O N I N E
```

Abundance	Happiness	Serotonin
Belonging	Healing	Soothing
Benefits	Kindness	Soulful
Charitable	Love	Stern
Comfort	Oxytocin	Superhero
Compassion	Peace	Trifecta
Dopamine	Proactive	Unity
Givers	Receive	Volunteer
Goodwill	Rene	
Gratitude	Rewards	

The Human Tribe

We are the same, you and me. All of us are comprised of an exquisite combination made up of oxygen, carbon, hydrogen, nitrogen, calcium, and phosphorus, sprinkled with the perfect dose of potassium, sulfur, sodium, chlorine, and magnesium. Every single one of us is made of these same glorious elements.

We may look different and we might act differently, but the essence of our being is exactly the same. Likewise, we experience the same feelings and our expressions carry a similar look. Sorrow and suffering look and feel the same for everyone and so do joy and happiness. We also want the same things. Every one of us wants to be loved, prosperous, safe, and seen for the beautiful creation that we are. We all want healthy children, fulfilling lives, and peaceful living.

There is no denying our sameness. We are profoundly interconnected. When we bleed, our blood is the same color. When we cry, the composition of our tears is the same. When we are touched deeply, our hearts warm with the same glow. Regardless of our gender, complexion, body type, sexual orientation, social status, religion, politics, or age, we are of the same tribe. We are the human tribe. If we have forgotten this, it is time to remember. In a world where polarization has taken center stage, we need to remember the truth.

At our core, we are truly one and the same.

—*Jane Harb*

Inspired Wisdom:

— — ——— ———————— —— ———————
———————— ——— —— ——— ————
—— ——— ——— ——— —————

```
H O N S T H H E S N O B R A C
A U P E A C E F U L D R F A C
R E E H W F E A E C N E S S E
B A N P O P E E R A A N V L R
P O T A S S I U M T O D E O I
F M F E J U P U R I S M R N L
E U N S T O H H X E E A E I B
U I T U S R S E O N D G A T T
T C Y O J E L U T R O N N R S
T L H I E P N S L R U E E O C
R A O R M S W I D P G S D G R
I C E O B O D Y P Y H I W E E
B A C L L R H R X P U U E N A
E L L G T P H O E M A M R S A
B L O O D E N I R O L H C M E
```

Blood
Body
Calcium
Carbon
Chlorine
Complexion
Elements
Essence
Gender
Glorious

Glow
Happiness
Harb
Hearts
Human
Hydrogen
Jane
Joy
Loved
Magnesium

Nitrogen
Oxygen
Peaceful
Phosphorus
Potassium
Prosperous
Safe
Sodium
Sulphur
Tribe

End Game

Spending time together with our sixty contributing authors inspires us in so many ways. Inspiration comes in many shapes, sizes, colors, flavors, and forms. Here is a patchwork word quilt with pieces taken from the puzzles, stories, and chapters to remind us of our journey. Collected here together, they read as a poetic message for us all.

We are the human tribe.

We are the fortunate ones.

Life, thankfully, has no one right answer. Our quest here is to learn and grow. What inspires you? What are you curious about? What's your joy? Say yes to it.

Only you have the power to take that leap of faith and soar to your highest potential.

Trust that your unique gifts make an impact on this world every day. Your happiness directly helps others be happy. Just as you are inspired by the outlook of others, humanity is all the more vibrant when you add your story to the multitude. Live a life you love.

You matter.

Life's decisions can be like flipping a coin. Heads or tails? It's your call. When we take responsibility for our lives, we are choosing to step into the light and shine. Let the light within come out to play. Givers receive the most. To live the best and most abundant life, rewrite the script to match inner beauty. Boldly step forward.

Walking your true path takes constant courage on the journey to genuine freedom. The authentic self is powerful and potent. When we emanate from our strengths, we become even more incredible, positive, loving, and productive people. We all soar on the wings of our passion. I hope your heart-centered authentic self is engaged in a spirit-filled endeavor that lights up your world.

Let tranquility refresh your spirit. Listen to the sounds of silence and connect deeply within yourself. Immerse yourself in the profoundly mystical power of the invisible world. You have control of your inner universe. Everyone has a shaman within.

It is in our connection that we find solutions, guidance, beauty, and love. Love your neighbor by loving yourself, and you will save the world. Surround yourself with people who want to see you grow. Get buff on the workout machine of life and pump up your soul muscles. When we remember, we can hone our skills.

Have love, compassion, and patience for yourself.

Practice gratitude every time you eat, no matter what you eat, as a reminder that the Earth sustains you. Celebration is an important key to happiness and resilience. Mother Earth is infinite in her wisdom. Take a look through animal eyes.

No mud, no lotus.

Look for magic in your day today. Believe in miracles and angels and synchronicity and dreams. Capture and savor heart-warming moments that immerse you in joy.

We are both infinite and infinitesimal. We are the sum total of all that we have experienced. Breathe in deeply your magnificence. (Are you still breathing through your nose?)

Listen.

Remember something joyful from your childhood. Go out and do something today that allows your inner child's curiosity to live in full expression. Experience and enjoy life to its fullest. Play!

Change begins with you and me. Focus on what you can do, not what you can't. Forgiveness is the root of compassion. Change is a journey best navigated from the heart. Every year represents a fresh start and renewed hope. Cultivating and fostering our hope supports our personal, professional, and spiritual growth. Open yourself to opportunities. Expand your horizons.

Above all, be kind.

The Universe thought you were a great idea. Be patient with yourself and others. Choose happiness, abundance, love, and health. Choose your highest destiny. Let yourself live an inspired life.

Make love your legacy. Merry Christmas spirit all year.

Thank you for being you and sharing your bright light with the world.

Sending you kind intentions of much love and many blessings.

May you flourish in joy, in love, in all that lights up your beautiful heart.

Tag! You're it! Go be awesome!

Meet the Authors

This collection of inspired wisdom messages emerged from the hearts, minds, and spirits of this fascinating variety of brilliant contributing authors.

Each contributor is listed in order of appearance by puzzle number. More information about these amazingly wonderful authors is available at www.InspiredWisdomWordSearch.com.

Foreword: Dave Farrow is the two-time Guinness World Record Holder for greatest memory. To earn this title, Farrow recalled the exact order of 59 decks of shuffled playing cards using the Farrow Memory Method. This method was originally invented to combat Farrow's dyslexia and ADHD and is now a unique memory system backed by a double-blind neuroscience study from McGill University. Today, Farrow uses his keen understanding of the brain in the public relations and media sector. He is the founder of BrainHackers.com and the CEO of Farrow Communications, a full-service marketing firm known for unforgettable branding. www.BrainHackers.com

1. Lisa Tansey is a biologist, computer scientist, musician, and lifelong student of politics, economics, and sociology. She is currently working on a science fiction novel where the artificial intelligences come to consciousness, appreciate the humans for creating them, and offer to partner with us to save the world for everyone. To read that story, email AwareLisa@gmail.com.

2. Crystal Lindsey, MBA, is a former foster youth, Fortune 500 professional public speaker, and entrepreneur. She helps others live an authentic and joyful life as a business and life strategist. Crystal leverages her expertise as a public speaker, emcee, corporate trainer, inspirational speaker, panel guest, and social media consultant. Crystal cofounded the nonprofit The Fostered, where her passion is to spearhead public speaking events and workshops to change the way foster youth learn. Contact her at Crystal@333SocialMedia.com.

3. Maria Dowd's signature My Amazing LYFE Map program is an interactive and holistic life-planning system that includes coursework, personality assessments, action planning, community support, and more to help women (and men!) powerfully navigate and activate transformative life goals and strategic game plans. The takeaway is a soul-stirring, whole-life blueprint with action steps and coaching on the road to greater success and happiness. Get your free 365-Day Self-Care Guide at www.MyAmazingLyfe.com/Self-Care-Guide.

4. Gerlando Compilati. I was born in Italy. My passion for travel has taken me to many beautiful and amazing places around the world. I have been fortunate enough to have met an eclectic group of people throughout my life. They have influenced and inspired me in so many ways. I started my own business importing from Bali, Indonesia, about thirty years ago, www.PurestEnergy.com. I am also a professional musician and visual artist living in southern California. View my art at: www.Flipsnack.com/Gerlando1/Gerlando-Compilati-S-Art-Gallery.html.

5. Dahlia Suiter is Stanford University bound. In her free time, she likes reading, writing, and creating music. She is passionate about creating positive change in the world around her and hopes that her words may inspire and spark curiosity in those who read them. Contact her at DahliaSuiterr@gmail.com.

6. Captain Dennis Daoust. I started sailing at age eight. After earning Public Administration and Sociology degrees from San Diego State University, I started a boat-building company. I later changed course and became a professional captain. I've owned *Scrimshaw*, a forty-foot sailboat, for forty-three years and have visited many places by sea and lived to tell my story. In my retirement, I play a little golf, founded the Borrego Springs Yacht Club, and sail my boat. You can contact me at CaptainHavoc@earthlink.net.

7. Maura A. Finn is a poet/writer, teacher, yoga instructor, energy psychologist, and transformational empowerment guide. Her passion for healing the human heart has led her all over the world where she has gathered experience as medicine. She is dedicated to helping others achieve their maximum potential through integrated creative healing approaches, starting with deep inner knowledge. She is also the author of *Architect of the Divine: Restoring the Heartspace for Love.* Visit her at www.FinnEvolutions.com.

8. Izzi Tooinsky is a unique vaudevillian entertainer who has been performing at fairs, festivals, schools, and museums since the dawn of time. Juggler, clown, comedian, storyteller, and educator, National Public Radio calls him the "wonderful, wandering, wizard of wisdom." Izzi is the author of two books, creator of seven storytelling CDs, father of two wild women, and has performed in seventeen countries around the world. Learn more about Izzi at www.IzziTooinsky.com.

9. Anna Pereira is the founder of TheWellness Universe.com (WU). As an agent of change and inspiration, Anna had a vision in 2013 to create WU for people changing the world. WU has been the global resource for seekers of well-being to connect to authentic people, content, classes, products, and services that help them live a better life.

10. Geraldine Gehrke Schwartz is an artist who lives in upstate New York. She enjoys cooking (and eating delicious foods!), golfing, square dancing, and walks along the Erie Canal. Among her many blessings are her three wonderful children, a loving and devoted husband, and trips to many a foreign land. She hopes to inspire others to invite more joy into their lives.

11. Bertha Edington has more than a twenty-year career in directing corporate and marketing communications with a variety of national business-to-business companies and multinational corporations. Founder and president of Marketing Influence, her powerfully effective programs have significantly contributed to increasing market awareness and the success of many organizations. Bertha serves on the board of directors of Walden Family Services. She is fluent in Spanish, an enthusiastic world traveler, and theater and arts supporter. Contact Bertha at www.GetMarketingInfluence.com.

12. Maryann Sperry is a graphic design artist for authors and speakers. Her business, Creative Marketing Café, provides book covers and interiors plus a variety of marketing materials. She holds bachelor's degrees in education and business with advanced training in web design, social media, and graphic design. Maryann volunteers for numerous nonprofit organizations, including the American Association of University Women (AAUW) and the Boulder chapter of the Society for Scientific Exploration. Contact Maryann at MaryannSperry123@gmail.com or you can learn more at www.CreativeMarketingCafe.com.

13. Kim Kinjo lives in northern California in the foothills of the Sierra Nevada mountains. Through her study of herbs, she was led into Ayurveda, the ancient, holistic medicine of India. As a master practitioner and educator, Kim loves to balance the healing arts with the performing arts. She enjoys singing, dancing, and performing. Her private practice is Kim Kinjo Ayurveda, www.KimKinjo.com. She is a member of an innovative, integrative online telemedicine group alongside medical doctors, www.ReachAyush.com.

14. Ingrid Coffin is the creator of inspirational Meta-Thoughts® messages, coauthor of *The Word Search Sage: Yoga for the Brain,* and founder of the Blue Sky Ranch community in Lakeside, California. Ingrid is also an esoteric life coach and evolutionary astrologer. Sign up at Ingrid's website to learn more and receive your free subscription to Meta-Thoughts at www.IngridCoffin.com.

15. Nick DeVincenzo, senior instructor and manager of the White Dragon Martial Arts School of East County in San Diego, California, has been studying martial arts since 1998. Nick has been teaching martial arts since 2001. A student of life on all levels, Nick can be reached at WhiteDragonOfElCajon@gmail.com or at www.WhiteDragonMartialArts.com.

16. Jayne Sams, EdD, is retired after twenty years of teaching and fourteen years as a school administrator to travel, garden, read, be with friends and family, and seek the "what's next" with an open heart. Practicing tai chi, going to the Y, and maintaining her properties in San Diego and beach house in Mexico has kept this traveler busy between excursions around this beautiful planet. Blessed with two grown children who don't object to her company, she skips from pillar to post wringing the best out of what life has to offer. Contact Jayne at JayneSams1@mac.com.

17. Brittany Lee is a newly published contributing author, with this being her debut. Alternative healing has inspired her to write about personal experiences and knowledge, bringing a better awareness to natural therapies, remedies, and lifestyles. You can find her spreading positivity on social media, sharing kindness for free, via Twitter and Instagram: @itsblee1234.

18. Darity Wesley, award-winning, bestselling author, lawyer, speaker, "Death Diva," and "Modern Day Oracle," has travelled the spiritual, metaphysical, esoteric, and personal development paths for many decades. She has become an extraordinary spiritual teacher and powerful resource for the application of evolving consciousness, which so many on this planet are experiencing at this time. Her Love from the Lotus World messages go out to her international community monthly, for free. Visit her website at www.DarityWesley.com to join.

19. Shelley Hines is the founder of Astrology Shines and currently serves as a lifestyle consultant. Using her gifts, talents, skills, and education as a master evolutionary astrologer, clinical certified hypnotherapist, Reiki practitioner, certified nurse-midwife, and registered nurse, she has served thousands of clients in the U.S. and abroad since 1994. Her passions include lifelong learning, teaching, and serving in diverse healing ways. Shelley may be contacted at AstrologyShines@gmail.com or www.AstrologyShines.com.

20. Patrick Oliver is a glider pilot, teacher, and scientist. He got his first glider ticket in the '70s. He flew microlights and gliders in England in the '80s and lived and worked on Kwajalein in the Marshall Islands as a sailmaker. He recently purchased a Schweizer 126 glider/sailplane and is looking forward to getting back into the sky. Contact him at Oliver.Aero@gmail.com.

21. Billiekai Boughton passionately serves as the board president of the San Diego Women Veterans Network and is the board secretary for Unity San Diego. She's a poet and the veteran section editor of the *San Diego Poetry Annual*. She and her son, Solomon, are currently writing and illustrating a book to support and encourage happiness for autistic children, titled *The Magic Four*. Reach Billiekai at www.SDWVN.org.

22. Barbara Eldridge has built a solid reputation as a success strategies specialist, coach, and speaker within industry and business for over thirty-five years. She is president and founder of Mind Masters, an organization for small business owners that encourages, challenges, and stimulates business development, financial growth, and personal and professional change. Her unique message helps entrepreneurs and small business owners meet the challenges of the changing marketplace. Reach out to Barbara at www.MindMasters.com.

23. Camille Leon is the founder of the Holistic Chamber of Commerce and the author of *False Starts: the misadventures of transformation*. Camille is available as a speaker, emcee, and consultant. Contact Camille at www.HolisticChamberofCommerce.com or connect at www.CamilleLeon.as.me.

24. Dr. Laurie Mastrogianis is a psychologist and author of the book *Shine On with STARS of Wellness: Stress Tension Anxiety Recovery System for Whole Person Healing*. Founder and executive director of the STARS of Wellness center in Sterling Heights, Michigan, Dr. Laurie is a living example of the transformational power of whole person healing. She has been specializing in helping others navigate their wellness journeys since 1989. Go to www.StarsOfWellness.com to receive your free STAR of Wellness.

25. Mara Clear Spring Cook has been a shamanic practitioner and teacher since 2008. Her training includes studies with Michael Harner's Foundation for Shamanic Studies as well as Katie Weatherup's Spiral Wisdom shamanic rraining program, and the installation of the Munay-Ki rites as taught by Dr. Alberto Villoldo. As a Reiki Master Teacher, she represents multiple lineages. Contact Mara for soul retrieval, shamanic healing, chakra balancing and more at www.MaraClearSpring.com or by email at Mara@MaraClearSpring.com.

26. Ariann Thomas, B.S., J.D., the author of *Changing Our Genetic Heritage: Creating a New Reality for Ourselves and Future Generations* (2018) and *Healing Family Patterns: Ancestral Lineage Clearing for Personal Growth* (2012), is an international healer, teacher, ceremonialist, speaker, and shaman. Her primary practice is Ancestral Lineage Clearing, a shamanic method to heal generational family wounds. Register for a gift, her blog, and information at www.AncestralLineageClearing.com.

27. Paula Wansley is an artist, freelance virtual business support provider, and subtle energy intuitive. She has many hats in her freelance career closet including web design, graphic design, creative consulting, photography, video editing, self-publishing assistance, editing, property management, bookkeeping, and general small business assistance. She is also a paralegal and an award-winning motivational speaker. Visit her website at www.LightShiningThrough.com.

28. Doveina Serrano is a master's-level therapist who enjoys doing tarot card and intuitive readings, energy healings, and life coaching. She likes to combine the latest neuroscience and holistic/intuitive techniques. Doveina is able to see how to enhance a particular people system that is broken. She is living her best life in sunny San Diego, California. To get help to create a new neuropathway, contact Doveina.Serrano@gmail.com or learn more on social media @DoveHelps or www.DoveHelps.com.

29. Shari Alyse has spent her life learning how to love herself fully and completely, motivated by her own journey through childhood sexual abuse and other childhood traumas. Shari helps women and men discover their joy by reconnecting them back to themselves through the practice of self-love. Shari is a motivational speaker, self-love coach, and author. She is the cofounder of the Wellness Universe, a community of world-changers who are helping the world become happy, healthy, and whole. Connect with her at www.TheWellnessUniverse.com.

30. Cheryl Marks Young is a coach, management consultant, growth strategist, award-winning author of *Love Your Life*, coffee lover, kitchen chemist, and food allergy awareness advocate. She creates solutions to help individuals survive and thrive in all aspects of their personal and professional journeys. Cheryl is the founder of Creative Blueprints for Leaders and The Allergy Ninja. Contact Cheryl and take the quiz to learn how to create the life you want to live at www.CreativeBlueprints.com.

31. Susan Sokol Blosser, wine industry pioneer, community leader, environmental advocate, and author, is a contemporary Oregon icon. Her most recent books are *The Vineyard Years: A Memoir with Recipes,* and *7 Lessons at 70: Notes from the Front Line.* She and her winemaker husband share their home at Sokol Blosser vineyard with two Tibetan terriers and two cats.

32. Denise Lewis Premschak is the founder of Field Guide, LLC. After a rich career as CEO for leading-edge international consciousness and wellness organizations, she currently serves on nonprofit advisory boards, and as an advocate for the end-of-life doula profession, health freedom, and the advancement of natural healing approaches in national health policy. Denise is a certified Sacred Passage Doula, Light Therapist and Introspect Leader Trainer, Reiki Master, BioGenesis Master, and dowser. Contact her at Denise@DLPrem.co.

33. Dennel Tyon is a doctoral student, mother, grandmother, minister, and caretaker at Kuddley Kritters Animal Rescue in Venus, Texas, who spends sleepless nights writing. An insomniac by nature, Dennel has written most of her life; she started journal-keeping at the age of thirteen. Curious about life and nature, Dennel has investigated and continued learning throughout her lifetime while working various jobs. She has raised four children to adulthood and has five beautiful grandchildren. Contact her at authdbtyon@gmail.com or learn more at www.MiddleGroundPublishing.org.

34. Diana Borges releases blockages and broadens perceptions so you can live a healthy and successful life. She empowers others with their innate knowledge and strength as well as their connection to their heart, soul, and Universe. Diana also assists with global awareness through Whole Earth Hub, a place for all to connect. She is a certified Life Purpose Coach, certified energy healer in multiple modalities, speaker, channeler, and author. Diana's websites are www.BorgesExperience.com and www.WholeEarthHub.com. Contact her at Diana@BorgesExperience.com.

35. Sarah Burchard is a natural foods chef, freelance writer, event coordinator, marketer, and certified health coach. She is an advocate for family farms and embodies the phrase "support local." In addition to supporting small wellness-based businesses, writing for local publications, and hosting farm-to-table events, she leads farmers' market tours in Honolulu, Hawaii. Learn more about Sarah at www.SarahBurchard.com or visit her blog www.HealthyLocavore.com. Connect with her on Instagram and Facebook at @healthylocavore and @yearofingredients.

36. Nadia Kim is an intuitive who uses her perceptions to help people live healthy and successful lives. She is an alchemist and channeler of unconditional love. Her mission is to be a beacon of positive energy helping tip the scales from survival mode to truly living. Download and subscribe to her free podcast, *Spiritual Tools for Your PHYSICAL Existence*, on iTunes, Google Play and Spotify, and check out her website, www.NadiaKimCoach.com.

37. Jennifer Whitacre is an empowerment strategist, a trauma specialist, and host of the *Yes, And...* podcast. Jennifer is skilled at helping her clients move beyond the self-sabotaging habits and knee-jerk reactions that keep them stuck and feeling lost. She has both the education and the life experience to help her clients move through their stuck places and fears, to find peace and fulfillment. Find Jennifer online at www.JenniferWhitacre.com.

38. Elizabeth Kipp is a health facilitator specializing in stress and chronic pain management, addiction recovery, meditation, and yoga. She is a bestselling author, certified Kundalini Yoga Teacher, Ancestral Clearing Practitioner, and Bilateral EFT/Tapping Practitioner, focusing on helping people actualize their inherent healing. Elizabeth works to help others achieve the same healing for themselves. Contact Elizabeth at www.Elizabeth-Kipp.com.

39. I'm **Janette Stuart**, Emissary of Joy at Angel Angles, which exists to spread more love, joy, and peace into the world. Angel Angles also shares the Divine beauty which resides within us all, helping us remember what beautiful, loving, amazing people we are and what a beautiful, loving world we live in. Find me online at www.Angel-Angles.com.

40. Kiva is a freelance writer, proofreader, lyricist, and poet. She has a degree in professional writing and specializes in medical terminology. Her background in production, networking, and organization of community events helps her as a singer, musician, miniaturist, artist, and health and well-being enthusiast. She has a passion for healing, peace, beauty, and deep spiritual connections. Ever eager to learn, she lives in deep gratitude for experience and opportunities to share with others. Yay, God. Contact Kiva at kivasama@sbcglobal.net.

41. Valerie Costa is the Special Sections Manager of *The Union* newspaper and the administrator of her county's tourism website, www.GoNevadaCounty.com. She took her own leap of faith six years ago to move to a town where she knew no one and had no job, and has been rewarded with a life beyond her wildest dreams. She can be reached at ValerieCassity@gmail.com.

42. Angelica Martinez has been a spiritual student since she was twenty-three, when a book on intuition fell off a shelf in front of her at her favorite bookstore. A massage therapist and educator since 1999, she's created the Healers Who Thrive community to help energy healers and massage therapists create their dream businesses using modern digital marketing techniques. Check it out at www.HealersWhoThrive.com.

43. Eve Wilson's passion is the healing and ascension of life on Earth into unity with our true selves. Her work is recognized by an international award for her *Weekly Word for Healing & Ascension* blog as "One of the Best Healing Blogs on the Planet" and as a "Master Healer" by UCM, who certifies her graduates nationally as Legal Healer Practitioners. Visit Eve for events, classes, healings, blogs, articles, Monday Prayers, and Wednesday Blessings at www.SpiritualHealers.com.

44. Dr. Ram Sharma is an accomplished poet and writer both in English and Hindi. His reviews, translations, articles, and poems appear in esteemed journals, magazines, and newspapers of India and abroad. Ram has to his credit eight poetry volumes. Editor in chief of two international journals, *RUMINATIONS* and *GLIMPSES*, Dr. Sharma serves as associate professor and head of the Department of English at J.V. College, Baraut, Baghpat, and U.P. in India. Contact him at Dr.RamSharma 777@gmail.com.

45. Lauren McCall. As an animal communication instructor, most of what Lauren McCall does involves the inner journey that people and animals take as they come together on their earthly and spiritual life paths. Through workshops, books, and lectures, Lauren travels the world sharing how the differences between our cultures and species tend to fade away when the common language of love and compassion is used. To learn more about Lauren's work, visit www.IntegratedAnimal.com.

46. Teresa Helgeson CHT, RMT, is the creator of Plant Music Therapy™, a new form of sound healing using plants connected to a system that lets the plant play music and become a musician. She has conducted several studies on the healing effects that music has on the body, mind, and spirit. Some of the benefits include boosts to the immune system, stimulated circulation, as well as reduced stress, anxiety, and depression. Get your free Plant Music Therapy™ download at
www.PlantMusicTherapy.com.

47. Dr. Paul Rudy is a composer, photographer, dreamer, creator, and traveler who has won international recognition. He has been called the "High Priest of Sound," and his music, the "universe unfolding one sound at a time." He is the Curators' Distinguished Professor at the University of Missouri, Kansas City Conservatory of Music and Dance, has a sound healing and meditation practice, and makes land art visible from Google Earth. Please visit at www.PaulRudy.net.

48. Thea Wirsching is an evolutionary astrologer with a strong focus on healing past-life wounds. One of her specialties is the Ceres reading or "food tour" of your birth chart, which is designed to help clients who suffer from eating disorders and body image dysmorphia. Thea is also the creator of a tarot deck based on her PhD dissertation, the American Renaissance Tarot. Learn more about Thea at her website, www.ThePlutoBabe.com.

49. Taylor Wansley is a senior in high school. She aspires to be an elementary school teacher and work in special education. She is very active in her community and has volunteered over eight hundred hours of community service, earning her several Gold President's Volunteer Service awards. Her hobbies include singing, dancing, acting, doing pageants, playing the piano, song-writing, learning sign language, and perfecting the art of makeup.

50. Paul Diserio is a photographic image maker, a longtime resident of Japan, and a world traveler. His professional work has taken him to many parts of Asia, where he has been able to capture local life that is both personal and reflects his search for beauty and fulfillment. He can be contacted via email at Paul@spinfish.tv.

51. Loren Smith is known as San Diego's Surfin' Santa, one of America's best Santas. Engaging, animated, and full of spirit, he has delighted tens of thousands of folks on TruTv's *Santas in the Barn* (2015), at Sea World shows, and at special appearances nationwide. Truly one of a kind, Santa Loren has arrived via fire truck, jetpack, surfboard, and pirate ship singing all the way to keep the Christmas spirit bright all year long. Find him online at www.SanDiegoSanta.com.

52. Dr. Wendy Mears-Kaveney is a founder and director of operations of SOUL Charter School, board member of Conscious Humanity, and managing director of Center of Love groups nationwide. She provides expert, personalized service in her many roles aligned with her passion and purpose. Wendy is the author of *It's My Story and It's Sticking to Me*™. With high ethics, integrity, dedication to excellence, and love, she generously shares her wisdom with others. Contact her at WendyKaveney@gmail.com.

53. Melissa Morgan is an innovative harpist and composer and deep believer in magic and mystery. She has a number of harp recordings and likes to play and work with crystals too. Her Etsy stores are HealingRocks.etsy.com and MyBlueMermaid.etsy.com. Her websites are www.MMMHarp.com and www.HealingRocks.info, For music or magic, contact Melissa at MMHarp@gmail.com.

54. Alessandra Gilioli is an international intuitive teacher, author, and visionary artist. She is the creator of the Galactic Oracle Cards sold in thirty-three countries and translated into three different languages. Alessandra leads retreats at sacred sites around the world. Sparkle your soul identity with tribal wisdoms, futuristic spiritual technologies, and enhance your multidimensional talents with free meditations at www.AlessandraGilioli.com.

55. Amalia Scott is a writer, counselor, and an evolutionary astrologer trained by Steven Forrest. Amalia is a mentor to many clients, offering intuitive, heart-centered reflection and guidance to individuals who seek to live the most fulfilled versions of their lives. You can reach Amalia with inquiries or to schedule readings with her via email, amaliava@gmail.com, or through her website, www.TheHareInTheMoon.com. You can read her regular astrological writings on Instagram, @thehareinthemoon.

56. Kaley Elizabeth Oliver is on the road to find out what's next. A recent graduate of Smith College with a degree in English Literature and minor in Jewish Studies, she is dedicated to living and speaking her truth, no matter what. Kaley writes poetry and fiction, loves exploring and learning, and is passionate about nature and wildlife. Contact Kaley at KaleyOliver96@gmail.com.

57. Simon Spalding is a musician, historian, and educator. He has performed and lectured at festivals, concerts, and museums throughout North America and Europe. He served as crew member aboard two schooners, a sloop, a barque, a brig, and the Polish vessel *Zawisza Czarny*. Simon's writings include articles, museum manuals, a play, and *Food at Sea: Shipboard Cuisine from Ancient to Modern Times*. Simon lives in New Bern, North Carolina, with his wife Sara and their two children. Find him online at www.TheMusicalHistorian.com.

58. Gigi Accomazzo is a sixteen-year-old high school student. Dedicated to inspiring the community to live more sustainable and eco-friendly lives, she has a nonprofit business that sells products aiming to reduce the use of single-use plastics. You can visit her website, www.HappyEarthDayToYou.com, or contact her at HappyEarthDaytoYou@gmail.com.

59. René Stern is a leading advocate for holistic wellness and vice president of sales and business development at Salt Chamber. A native Floridian, she's been intrinsically motivated to passionately volunteer her entire life to purposefully impact humanity. René serves on the advisory board for the Cystic Fibrosis Foundation of South Florida and as founding president of the Boca Raton Holistic Chamber of Commerce. Through thirty years of philanthropic leadership, René has helped raise well over $1 million. Contact her at ReneStern@icloud.com.

60. Jane Harb is a yoga and meditation teacher at the University of California, San Diego. She has certifications in yoga, children's yoga, Thai massage, Reiki, and yoga for trauma and PTSD. In addition to teaching at UCSD, Jane works with private clients and also teaches yoga classes and stress reduction for veterans and active-duty personnel. She can be found on the web at www.YogiJane.com.

Now that you've met the individuals, here are some interesting statistics about the group and the book.

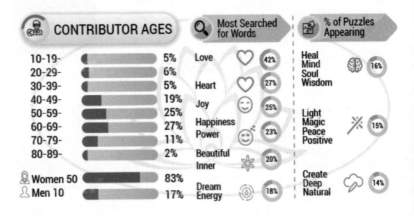

CONTRIBUTOR AGES		Most Searched for Words		% of Puzzles Appearing	
10-19-	5%	Love	42%	Heal Mind Soul Wisdom	16%
20-29-	6%				
30-39-	5%	Heart	27%		
40-49-	19%	Joy	25%		
50-59-	25%			Light Magic Peace Positive	15%
60-69-	27%	Happiness	23%		
70-79-	11%	Power			
80-89-	2%	Beautiful Inner	20%		
Women 50	83%			Create Deep Natural	14%
Men 10	17%	Dream Energy	18%		

If you have a story, poem, or wisdom you want to share, please consider being a *Yoga for the Brain* contributing author. Find out how to apply at www.YogaForTheBrainAuthor.com.

Answers

No Mud, No Lotus

1. We Are the Fortunate Ones

```
TTOHATESNUSBKPE
CHOCOLATESTLIET
CPMNIESAHSDEAAP
OILGAWLOSCYSTCY
MSHEITAOAIASPHG
MTUTARUNPTLIREE
UECSASSRCOINASF
NHTHHWUEEIDGHOO
IEPSEIRREBWARTS
CWDRGYHREITEES
ALSAENETNTUCNRR
TROSNWIELNDICNE
EJNVOOBMAAMLIYW
LAUHECMTRSEKSKO
TYSYODEEAASWUUL
POPCORNJLAWRMEF
```

2. You Matter

```
SUTRENDSRIPPLES
PNSSLUFGNINAEMW
LIYEPOSITIVELYE
EQOIGLEARNEDUAP
HUPRRAGRATEFULT
GEOEEERBLISCMYP
OOWVRGOUTIUUFFF
OAEONNNTOLNURIO
DARCENDATCLDATC
CRYSTALIHLNNSNU
TINISPVIYCREAES
HTIDHAPPINESSDY
GGIFTSTCAPMIOIN
ITREFLECTRETTAM
ROSECNEULFNIALL
```

3. Truths to Tell

```
PSUOIROLGCBFRPA
PURSUEVOLFOUTRB
EDRCOURAGELLAOO
SUWPTLISTFDLUPT
NLAQOAIAPELYPEP
ONBDDSVGSIYOENI
ILUEGIEEHARNTSR
SGNITARGETNILIC
SSDCTVOVUYNUTTS
AWAKENINGTMERII
PENSTSIHAISVSES
HTTSNTUINCTEASM
YOOAYUROJAOIBYA
ANPSHTURTPRHDIE
NXNEESRBEACUTR
EYFREELYMCRAYSD
```

4. Say Yes to Life

```
CTHGEITALIIPMOCU
HYUECOUSINSNIEN
OTHRILLVERRSACC
PIYLIMAFEYLATIL
SROALLAPXNGUATE
YOGNSNAICISUMCS
EIJDAPSKILLSHAE
NROOSCSFTMIAURS
OESWYDIIECLFHPX
MFECNOARMLNNEEE
CNJERUTNEVDAATL
SIIONUMNNMKSVBP
ERYTBOGUTSANEDM
FWSOREMBRACINGO
PLAYNGDYDNAHSC
```

5. Curiosity

```
APLACECRDAHLIAW
LESUOREDNOWAIEI
LSAEHUMANWPLACD
OEUFCUOLEROLPXE
WRYIFNOUURTRESC
CELETCEFLFECLOI
EHEXPERIMENTMDN
TLATTRRTRAAPHYV
IISNWTSULELRTOA
NRLAGAPAEEPINML
IDTTVIBEXCSXAHU
FATRRNNBCOAZEDA
NEYOJTFGICIRNLB
IECPTYSRYNAIBOL
URAMWEUSGOKMEME
NNOITCELLOCESSE
```

6. The Reach

```
SSECIOHCOMSDNIW
ERATINMTDENNISS
VESSELINSEMBSAE
SADERUTANULAIYG
HCOIUMRVTUOLENA
OHARRETIEPOAOBR
RHLOEESGARAIDHU
ISTEGACASFSCAIO
ZSKASSLTASNRHRC
ODYIASSEIOBEEEM
NOEFETOMIOMHEGE
VSEYOSUNRANTDNR
ECAUTIOUSTHOEAW
CREWIDRAWERMNDD
```

7. Wisdom of the Inner Child

```
W E N E R R B L I S S S E M E
E M B P U D D L E S P W E A R
A N L E T A R B E L E C O V
T R U S T E F Y O N A E O U R
I S P O P S I C L E S T M N N
E S A U C I N N E R H N P R C
H E R L H M N I Y U I E A L D
T N U E I O O C T P N S S E H
H T A I L N C D I D G S S A S
U H M J D K E L S G L S I T E
M G H O H E N J O I A I O O R
M I Y Y O T C I H W M N A F
I L I T F O H E A R T S P A C E
N Y O U D U S E U P E L T K R
G N I L I M S W C I S E E T H
I G N I V O L A U G H I N G N
```

8. The Power of Play

```
I T I U R F N C R E R E T A W
L I G H T A L A U G H T E R S
M H C U O T G S H S I E J P O
A Y A N O N D N E U H Z E E C
T B R A I N A E I O M C Z M R
U L T V N N R H C N I B O I E
R A L N S T G H D E R D L W A
E O L F K O I R S G S A S E T
S N U D Y L E L E I R S E W I
S N F I D L I T W D E H T L V
L L R R N O I T A N I G A M I
L H E E S P O M L I W E E R T
E N W E Y T I L A T V N O Y
C F O P P O E S I F T I V T E
P L P A Y W E N E R G Y A L P
```

9. Laugh, Dance, Sing, Play!

```
I A L P B F L S S D R A Z I L
S P L I O A I A P I E S P T O
U W L R M N R G U S Y E N U S
N E T A G L N E G G R F O T T
S M O T Y I F N F E H E I U S
H E A E L C U R I O S I T Y S
I B U G S L L R T H O E A J E
N O G Y I A A N E E D T N E C
E I P N T C H U E B S I I A N
G N I N J A A R Y S M A G M I
E I L D R E F L M R N E A E R
C M L L U F R E D N O W M B P
N E O R F M R O A M C M I E H
A I W P A R T I E S L D E H R
D S M I H W O O S K C O R M D
```

10. Inspiration

```
P P E E H S W E A S L E E P B
G O S E C R E T R E S E S O D
R S S I W N T G D M K O C R E
A K J I O I Y N E R D A H I N
T C T O T O L N U N Y U W R E
I O L U I I D E O F E A E K
T S D B Y D V I F I C E R E R
U E L Y L F R E T T U B T I H
D N D A G F G R S A A T Z T E
E A R E W O N D E R F U L A G
I E W T S M U D E I E F O S R
G O U A O S H A P P Y W R T L
N M O O R D B M S A N O E E
U Y D B L E E L E N J O Y L E
S S H C A E P S B I N G S F
```

11. Love Your Neighbor and Yourself

```
E R I S O B J E C T E N P C H
A V E N T V W M N G V E E E E
T H A L O H I A L E O I A L W
O R L S E I G S T A L G C T R
C D E S A N T U U E C H E T I
C O O H D Y T A O A R B F O N
A U F Y R T L L R H L O U B G
L S B F P E A S E I T R L Y B
T E M E E H M E S S P I L N G
K O C A T E D I A E S S Y I R
N C U R E I D A N N L L N N O
A D E C N R L O V D I D Y I H
I B N G H G D T O M E M N Y C
S E T Y O U R S E L F R A E N
L O A C T I O N S C A R E T A
N F Y G R E N E E S U F N I S
```

12. Simple Truths to Practice

```
E C E L E B R A T E C N U O B
N E T H E T A I C E R P P A E
I U N N V E L B I X E L F I V
V E M I S T A K E S T I M D A
I Y V R L N N A Y R A M R P S
D I D S E P U R P O S E O N I
D S U O I C I P S U A L E A G
A D C L B N T C H M O P M U H
S C E O U O T U S G O A T S T
G T C R N F H U I I Z T P E I
Y O R E A N E Z I E D U A F N
W E R E P P E T D T E A D U G
T R U S T T E C A N I M A L S
R E S P E C T R T R G O R E A
S P E R R Y H T P I G D N E A
```

13. Cultivate Inner Peace

```
B T R A N Q U I L I T Y R I S
N R E V I R G Y O X A L E R E
U M G N A T U R E H L R A W R
A I S N R S E W S N U T N E E
S K U S I T A E O N F O L O N
H E B R Y P R T U R I O U E E
E R L B I F P R T T T R E E M
A A I A E P T I A V U H C L W
R T M R H U P T D L A L Y A H
T O E T R X I L O O E B T H M
S J E E C D E O E A B E E N I
N N T E E R P E N S R D A I N
N I D M E T A V I T L U C P D
R K R E N N I E S P E A C E S
S A C R E D E Y L M L A C N T
```

14. The Mystery in Silence

```
J S U S N R E T T A P S T B N
S K E C S S A U S O U R C E A
E I N I A T N U O M T F M S T
H L E C Y N R O U C U E C A U
C L L O N E N E E O D E E T R
A S A F E M E N S I I L S E A
E T C F D N N S T E B I C U L
B O I I O O E A T I D N E C M
S N T N C R T M S H E G O H Q
S T S M E I E I O L G S A U K
E N Y I O V V S I T A U I R L
L T M N I N S S T W I E O C A
P A R K I E N O A S T O T H W
M T L I B R A R I E S H N E T
E Y G R E N E E P O R C H S R
T E I M M E R S E D I R G N I
```

15. Life Skills 101

```
I L O Z N E C N I V E D I E E
N S T R I V E C V A L U E R M
N R E A S Y T I R G E T N I A
E E N O H M T E S O F P P O S
R H A C C O U N T A B L E R T
T C U C P O N T R R A I D T E
I A E O E S N C C U I S M R
F E O N E E R S D N S B P M E
L T T F D I C I I C A L A O A
E K C I N T V I I S O S G L C
A Y Y D R I O P T Y T E W M H
R R Y E D V I S U C C E S S I
N O C N K I H O S I A E N N E
S M I C N T G R O W K R I T V
L E L E S C E H S W E E P V E
E M R Y D A C A Y U F G N U K
```

16. It's Your Choice

```
I M H E A L T H Y A T A E H W
K E E T I H W H D E C P I S I
G P O S I E M P O W E R E D N
N S O C N O N S S U C N U E P
I I S V O O U I S G O Y R D
P L E Y I A P N D N L H A A C
P H S O G T O S O C A Y T M J
I G U L O S I I E T E H I F E
L T L O R T T V B R E N C R A
F A P U A A N O E U U I P E S
C N O I T A T L U S N O C E M
T I L I E E M I E T S C T W A
I S D C D P N S H A P P Y A S
E E C I O H C H E A D S R Y S
M T O A S T G N I L I M S O N
```

17. Healing Happy

```
T M H O T E S D N I M S Y O J
U A R Y O G A Y G H Y T Y H B
S S A E G A N A M M C N E O D
E S Y A S A T S P T I A N T N
C A U I T T D T N E L C R O E
R G N T N T O R F I O L U E F
O E I C O M U R N O M R O Q I
F R U U S T A G A L C A J I T
B T Y P O F E L T T I U T C F
S Y E P H O L I S T I C S I I
A G N I A E R L D L C V I N V
U R R N C I V Y P P A H E O L
N E U G P R O C E S S M R E
A N S S T A N C L Y D O B H E
E E V I T I S O P L I F E C S
```

18. Hope

```
M P Y G E T A R T S T S O O B
Y O C E M E R G E H T N O P E
P W A P B L I M E L L O W F T
S E T O R S O C C A S I O N M
T R A H A E U M O P N T T R O
H S L C C U I S N T O C A I N
G E Y D E N I A T N I A M A N
U D S C D G N I R E T S O F A
O P T I M I S T I C A R W R R
H Y S D R O W Y B M D E E U T
T H T N O I T I U T N I S I R
O G N I T A V I T L U C L T U
G H N U R T U R E D O E E I V
E N T H E A T O U G F V Y O H
E S T T I M D E S Y G R E N E
```

19. Walk Your True Path

```
M T S O I R B Y E L T E H E E
R O E U E N E L A A X U N L M
E I D F O L D R A C N L S R T
O B F S L I T I E I I E E T S
L O R E I S R P V G C N U R E
L A H Y E W T E H I N E A F N
R S N C H I R T T I D T P S I
E E N T O S E A C S S U U S U
E A A N E N I N S N Y O A O N
G P A E S R L I N I M V L E
A L E W H T N M I R E T N P G
R W E B T R A U O C E V S A N
U A D O Y U H L B A B E A I A
O L R R M E G L H I N E S E D
C K M N S U O I C E R P O N H
S P A R K L Y A N C I E N T Y
```

20. The Long Glide Home

```
W L L E W D E E C N A D A W L
B L A E S A N C T U A R Y H T
S R M E L T E O M E A R E I S
O O O O R D N O R T R L N S A
H O N T I U E H E D O M P E
S G L L H N E G M A H I C E B
R E G I T E I L R E G G T R T
E H L A V L R C I H L I I E W
H W I G I E D S T F H E N H O
T N I W A R R Y N W T G O S N
A O T F E E G N I L C R I C D
E O U A S P A C E R O W S N E
F P M A S P A T R I C K I S R
I T I R I P S C L I M B V O N
```

21. Go Be Awesome!

```
G Y E R E H P S O T A R T S O
I U D O I O N S P V O B T U N
F E K E H N D E L O T O O O D
T O I S E S V N E L O U Y I V
S T N E M E L E A U M G R G A
U A D R O E I R S N T H E A L
O L N V S T H A E T P T C T U
R E E I E L H W K E I O O N E
E N S C W U K A R E T N R O R
N T S E A P I E N R I E G C A
E S T N G A T A Y K V L M A C
G Z A R O T N E M I Y I L N G
T O R B A A E A R E V O L I M
A Z S M I C N D G Y K C U L B
```

22. Live Strong

```
B R R A D I T N E M N G I L A
A E T E F R O P S T E S S A E
T I S M A T T R A C T E D N C
A N Y T O U O O R S T R H A N
L F E N M I G D T H I A S R E
E O T O V R G U E P N T S A S
N R E A N J O C O C C T C B S
T C H A R A C T E R R C G R E
B E L I E V E I S A E B N A V
B S T R O N G V T N D A I B L
P O S I T I V E T O I L V Y O
L O V I N G G U M E B A O N V
T F A R R I A O M A L N R L E
L L Y O E T A N A M E C P B R
O U W S E G D I R D L E M D O
P O W E R S S E C C U S I O C
```

23. The Love List

```
M S S M Y S U B S T L O B Y Y
L P O T I E C I O H C N V L E
L A I S L N C O M M U N I T Y
T C Y E N U D R E T I M C G H
A E E T R S S F S V A M N Y L
L I F E I A F E U F L I W I T
L H T Q H P D R R L T O E E E
O J O R U S I N I A N E S M L
W Y S E N I E D E E V E B I U
O F N A F L E R N L N R S T D
E W M D L I C T O E A D S S E
O U L I U T L V I C R C S O H
H N M N S E E L E O N E V E C
R A Y G P R I O R I T Y S D S
C S U P P O R T E A R T H A Y
```

24. Transformations

```
B P E A C E L I T E R A C Y H
O N M W H H E O H O M L E E P
D G R E U N A T V H A R A S E
Y I O E I P W N A E S R O N V
E L F H D O L P G S T W E E I
M A S L R I P I T E R M M M T
B L N G N I S I F E O S A S I
R L A H E M F N E T G G E L S
A A R R L E P S I Y I O B A O
C I T U N N S O H N A N I U P
E C N E L T N E E Y N O G R U
D O B R L A U T I R I P S I B
N S R I L L E G H T S E S E T
I Y G R E N E H Y H T A P M E
M L I W O N D E R F U L G H T
```

25. Listen to the Shaman Within

26. We Choose Our Destiny

27. Abundance and Possibility

28. Create

29. Let Your Soul Shine

30. Celebrate!

31. Inspiration from the Vineyard

32. Soul Evolution

33. Listen Within

34. Regain Your Power

35. Fluidity

36. Awareness and Self-Love

37. Childhood's End

```
H S E R C A T I H W W F L E S
E D U U F F U E S I E R I A N
A E G N E B U T T E R F L Y A
R G N C O Q E N H D E L S C W
D A H O I O E A E E O N K N P
Y R O N R S C U U W N N R T R
E U U D S E C O E T O T O P O
N O N I E C F D C W Y T I E F
W C A T E R P I L L A R R C O
T N I I T R H E N Y E U O C U
R E U O E R D A U N T V X A N
U T C N H G L U F R E W O P D
T E N A E M I T U N T J B L I
H I C L P S E N P O T E N T L
F M R O F S N A R T D L I H C
```

38. Keep Choosing Forgiveness

```
C T S E D R A H L L P A U S E
E O B T L T H E E I R N E B F
E P M R E I A C C F D E O I N
N F F E E Z T A E A R R G T
H O O O O A U A R G A S E N G
D R I S R R T S B D T N D N L
E W B S E G T H M E T T I I T
B A L E S A I E E L T S S E G
I R E N N A P V Y W O H N L N
W D S D W I P O E O F T O O R
T H I N O T I M H N E V C M E
F N R I D E K C O K E O U M T
G N I K E E S H E C L S P I N
S I D E O M I S T A K E S U T
```

39. Joy Is Your Birthright

```
B Y O S E G A S S E M U F A S
E R M E M E A T E N T L T P B
A N G E L S U N O T O L A I R
U V L E G A Y O O U T C U R I
T L A T R A E H R I E E I F G
I E N T O M N I P O T E N T H
F I O B N T S M J O C A Y A T
U A I S L H R A A N B G E P J
L N T T E E L E A Y N O E R V
S L I G H T S T A I H S E E C
R D D Q C A I S R S S T Y C H
E I N U R N A I E U C R I D
T O O F E E H K N N A R E O T
T H C H E S D C I G G M E U W
A G N I V R E S E D I V I S N
M I U E W O R L D T E N I H S
```

40. The Light Within

```
D A O R S H L E T E E M I N
D E E A Y O S O D U Y R L I
E C R V G H M T V I T A S A
I L O I W T A N E E S L L E
R O C K O O E E N L A N M P
R I D E H G R C G E G E I I
A S T E S E D S V N R N N O
C T U R C T H E T G O N I H
G E G F E H R N E S E L O S
N R P L B E U I L R S E E K
O E A E O R S M E C A L P B
S D A Y E W A U N I H T I W
R M O U N D D L S M I L E Y
O U S E A R C H I N G I V E
```

41. Take a Leap of Faith

```
L E N T A P E Z I N G O C E R
F P O W E R E A R L E H S S L
Y W N M O V I N G I A P M A C
N I P N T F A M I L I A R O T
H D R E A M E L L U N K N O D
W V O L U N T E E R I N G E N
W I F A E T N L S R T H L T F
A I I I N G R B R P I B T N H
H I T T I N Y A U O I E U E O
E R S N T E O T M S L R F L B
A C G E U S N R S S I D I A B
A S I T O P P O R T U N I T Y
H T W O R G P F F U L L E S T
J U O P V M Y M H I G H E S T
F C Y T I R C O I D E M U L S
H K E A T S O C R A Z Y A R T
```

42. Right at Home at Work

```
W A O R S R E P A I D K I S A
S T D A E E D G N I D E E W G
E F Z V A N G E L I C A O R Y
O U R E E P I A G A R D E N S
T S P I N N R U R A T R A E H
R S C S I I T A N U G R T U Y
A L E I N R T U C E O N U L O
I F E B T O O R R T G C E T J
M O N E Y N I V A E I P L Y H
A Y M K W L E S A M R C Y O S
O I S H I W P H S E R E E G O
T E O G O I U R T A D I N A U
D L H R R P A R T U P N G N L
E T K I L E V A R T A W E H I
S E T F U L F I L L E D L L T
```

43. Center on Your Inner Wisdom

44. Let's Live Life

45. Look Through Animal Eyes

46. Connection

47. Ode to Mother Earth

48. Food Wisdom for All

49. Beauty

```
R O L O C R O L Y A T T L E
E H F S N O R A C A M E D Y
N S R E B L M E A E E I W N
N U E U T U Y P D F S O A W
I N N R I F C I A N N T T H
I S C N U I S V I S U A L G
Y E H O S T U S I R S H I O
W T N U U U A N E E L I H O
E A M O S A C E T P H O O D
K I N D N E S S F E N E V N
B R I S R B G P O E T R Y E
H T E I L P S T S D O O F S
O F T A L E E T S D N U O S
L Y H O B B Y T U A E B O J
```

50. Zen and the Blossom

```
C A Y R R E H C S T E R C E S
P M T G U R S N L P E N A N C
D A S R A B O L H A E V G O E
R S H O E W L E A Z R A N R N
T T W V Y A M O Y T O I I R E
M E L E M E N T S I E C T S E
I R N S R G U E R S A P E Y R
P P M A D A S E C N O E E O U
M I L E E A S R O N I M L N T
T E N B J I N P E N E S F T C
L C T K D A Y C G D H S A A I
U E T I M M P E E R L O S S P
A S T O H S P A N S L E E E Y
P O U I N A J O N F E M A R F
H A N A M I W R E F L E C T Y
```

51. A Letter to You from Santa

```
T H H E L G R T E S A F T E A
Y R R E M O W S D G I R L S T
M P T G A I R I I J F I T S N
Y A O U N R K E O S D E S P A
G T G K E I T Y N P E N A R S
V I L I E V A R E I L D M E E
L E G A C Y E C G R I S T S L
O N V E R L N I C I G Y S E A
U C G E S A V A L T H O I N S
H E N E R I R O T E T B R T M
E N P E N E V R A N B D H L I
I O L G I E D R E A M S C S T
H O T E E C N E S E R P N I H
T W I S H E S F A M I L Y N G
```

52. The Power of Love

```
R M E V E U N I V E R S E R L
A E A Y T P H I N H N G I S O
D R P N O L A I T N E T O P V
I U O W I S S L I B E L V E E
A P E W H F A L E V E R I E M
N R N S W E E T N E S S B A W
T S E E W M A S G H E A R T C
C E V I T C A R T T A V A C R
E I S S A A A G N S E D T A E
C L Y T Y T L E N L I N I V A
M P A D E H C U O E A T O Y T
E I E F N A T U C D T T N G I
A T U H E E S L N R E I O R V
R L F P V O W U A R I O C E E
S U T N A R B I V E D C C N E
O M F L K A T R U T H O V E E
```

53. Believe in Magic

```
E C A E P O W E R M A N I F S
L C I E H S T E R U T A N M U
I H I G E E V E I L E B I N C
M E R M A I D S A Y N N U F O
S R N G R M S S E N D N I K F
M I A C T A S G L F E G S I C
C S G R H I P A U T R N E E N
S H R A L A I L A S N I I S E
T E O E R C N V T W E P N N V
R D M K E E I T E O S E N O A
A S I P S T J O I B S E E G E
N N S S L Y S S E N I P P A H
G A S U B L I M E I G N D R D
E E C L S T I B B A R I G D H
T I N L U N I C O R N S I F E
```

54. Soul Identity

```
A M A G N I F I C E N T W E H
L A V E T E B H E E S P O W R
L A E R Z W R V I Y D O B M E
O T L I H I I N R T S T U U A
W O R E I S L G N I I T N L S
T P E A S F L R G T P I F N O
I E Y A Q S I N U N V E E N N
L S M R H S A C R E D P P E G
O N S I T L N N R D O C U Y R
I E F E S S C S D I V O R L T
L T U P N I E U E R O L P X E
I T I O O T N P O F A L O O R
G V W E F O I R A B L A S T C
M A G I C A L W T T H E E W E
O T H G I L R C E L L S L D S
```

55. Tell Your Story

```
T W E R B E H E P R E W O P G
K N O W I N G N E S S J R L L
L Y O S B E W G R O U E O R I
M A G I C I A N C S D E T Y S
J O O R T U Y R E I A T W D T
O E O S G A E Y P O U I O E E
U V W N A A M S T G S N R H N
R O A N L T T R I D I I D S O
N L S I E I C E O I T F U E N
A F T O L I G M N F L N T M T
L Y E D A A A H S Y S I O N T
U C L M R E M A T T E N Y E O
O U A R B A D A C A R B A R C
A R T I S T L S P E A K I R S
A L U O S T H G I L E D F E T
```

56. Internal Authority

```
I A T S U O I C E R P M C O N
Y T S I N U L D A L L Y C H R
R T E R E E U E S C I H T E U
O A U P A T H W A Y S E W V N
T T Q A I A I N G R B S G I I
S I N T E R N A L A N A N T Q
K A L E Y B V I Z A B T I I U
R U A F L E X I B L E N T S E
M T G N I L L F L I E F O I
T H A N R E V I L O D E I P N
C O L L E C T I V E L Y L M N
P R S S E R G R O P O W P E E
R I I N R E S O U R C E U G R
I T N G N I N A E M B A R K T
E Y R C N A L S U C C E S S W
F R E E D O M O W O R G R L D
```

57. Some Words of Wisdom

```
N Y S I G W P G E R O L P X E
M O L E O A C O N E P O C S C
N S M R T R A Y N I S L S O A
V S D I E E O D N E D M A Y N
E S E A S D E M I T A L T N V
O N T E C A R B M E H U A T A
T E C J V T H O R S A S S P S
E E R O O C A D I E U E N M S
T N R U U Y A R B O U Y O O E
T S W R K R U R I Q D T I D F
E T O N I O A C E H E P S S I
L R R E N E G S E T M S I L
A W K Y D R I L E L R E A W F
P O L L P I M A G I N E P O W
```

58. We Can Change the World

```
S T E E P L A N E T Y H E A
R E G N A H C F T A T N D E
E A F B R A T O H A H R N V
E F O S P E C R L L G V H R
O L S U O L U C A R I M T E
G E D W I D T E O R M H E S
N T E H O C Y S O M E S E E
A I X N O N E N M L A Y T R
E L A M I W M L R L L Z E P
T T M T O E A E C L A A Z T
E O P R N G D R A Y K O M O
N E L T E U E C I R C E G S
S D E N C T O G E T H E R F
O R T E A L I M E S U E R T
A S R W E G A S E M O H O N
```

59. Givers Receive the Most

```
O S E R V O L U N T E E R V I
X C E E B X A C O M F O R T L
Y E R E N E L B A T I R A H C
T T V K B P L S R E V I G S O
O U S I A E G O O D W I L L M
C E N N E A N R N R E T S G P
I V C D D C H E E G L P R S A
N I Y N M E E H F S I A A G S
H T T E A K E R S I T N E N S
E C I S H D E E U I T V G I I
A A N S M W N P T A O S N H O
L O U I A I L U F L U O S T N
I R T R P Y D S B A N D O O U
N P D P R E N I M A P Q D O W
G S A T C E F I R T O R L S D
W H H Q L S E R O T O N I N E
```

60. The Human Tribe

```
H O N S T H H E S N O B R A C
A U P E A C E F U L D R F A C
R E E H W F E A E C N E S S E
B A N P O P E E R A A N V L R
P O T A S S I U M T O D E O I
F M F E J U P U R I S M R N L
E U N S T O H H X E E A E I B
U I T U S R S E O N D G A T T
T C Y O J E L U T R O N N R S
T L H I E P N S L R U E E O C
R A O R M S W I D P G S D G R
I C E O B O D Y P Y H I W E E
B A C L L R H R X P U U E N A
E L L G T P H O E M A M R S A
B L O O D E N I R O L H C M E
```

Gratitude and Appreciation

This book reflects the creation of unity through diversity. Sixty voices, one book. Wow!

We have mother and daughter contributors as well as three generations of family represented with mother, daughter, and granddaughter.

Our brilliant Puzzle Master is Rick Smith. He carefully crafted each supremely soul-satisfying puzzle and answer. Rick also designed the book, created the nine-pointed star image, and the whole brain illustration in "How to Play."

All puzzle-text Inspired Wisdom messages are © by the individual authors. They are used by permission.

Vast waves of appreciation to Paula Wansley for taking care of all of our contributing authors and a multitude of details.

A big shout-out of thanks and appreciation to our beta readers and supporters: Bertha Edington, Darity Wesley, Ingrid Coffin, Jill Daoust and Valerie Costa.

We are deeply grateful to our significant others Bill Jurel and Erika Gilmore for giving us a loving foundation of nourishing support. We appreciate you!

The award-winning *Yoga for the Brain* series is consistently excellent due to the expert editing of our editor extraordinaire Melissa Morgan. The loving care and attention she gives to each word and punctuation mark emanates from the pages. Here's her bio:

Growing up, I always wanted to be a writer, or maybe a librarian if the writing took a while. Even though I played the harp from a very young age, I didn't want the challenge of being a professional musician.

In college I studied writing and editing and had a career all planned out. I went to Guam and published my first book and stories. Then I became a music composer and my life trajectory changed. Nevertheless, I didn't stop writing, and continued to study editing and journalism.

I came to California to pursue my harp career as a composer, performer, arranger, teacher, touring musician, and recording artist. I never gave up my love of words, continuing to write and edit all the while.

After many other collaborations and a lifelong friendship, Cristina asked me to edit her *The Tao of Sudoku: Yoga for the Brain*, the first book in the *Yoga for the Brain* series. I've served as editor for all of these wonderful books. It has been a complete pleasure to work on these marvelous offerings, and return to my writing and editorial roots.

Biographies

Cristina and Rick Smith

Brother-and-sister team Cristina and Rick Smith have been solving puzzles together their whole lives. They spent their formative years playing games for hours upon hours, both inside at the table or on the floor and outside in the backyard. Though they have very different personalities and interests, Rick and Cristina were able to meet over a game of cards or a jigsaw puzzle and happily hang out together, much to the delight of their parents.

Rick has been creating games, riddles, and puzzle books for decades. Cristina's writings have appeared in scores of magazines, newspapers, newsletters, websites, and books. In this book, Rick is the puzzle master and book designer and Cristina is the wordsmith and project orchestrator.

Their signature *Yoga for the Brain* series of profound philosophy and fun puzzles books have earned numerous awards and accolades, including Gold Medal Winner for Best Book Series from the Council of Visionary Resources.

Rick lives in Colorado and is retired from a life in high-tech and startup companies. Cristina lives in northern California, is the founder of the Subtle Energy Center, and has served in numerous community and nonprofit organizations.

When they get together, Cristina and Rick still enjoy doing jigsaw, word, and logic puzzles as well as cooking a delicious meal.

Learn more at www.YogaForTheBrain.com.

Yoga for the Brain Books
by Cristina and Rick Smith

www.YogaForTheBrain.com

Animal Wisdom Word Search: Yoga for the Brain *with Lauren McCall*
The Word Search Sage: Yoga for the Brain *with Ingrid Coffin*
The Word Search Oracle: Yoga for the Brain *with Darity Wesley*
The Tao of Sudoku: Yoga for the Brain

Do you have a wonderful story, poem, or wisdom message to share?
Would you like to be a *Yoga for the Brain* contributing author?
Find out how at www.YogaForTheBrainAuthor.com.

Thanks for Playing!

Inspired Wisdom Word Search  **185**